The Book On

Men (for Women)

A Woman's Guide to Understanding Modern Men

The Book On Series

Megan Rios

Published by The Book On Publishing, 2025.

First edition. October 27, 2025

Website: https://thebookon.ca

Substack: https://thebookonpublishing.substack.com/

The Book On Men (for Women): A Woman's Guide to Understanding Modern Men

First edition. October 27, 2025

Copyright © 2025 The Book On Publishing

ISBN: 978-1-997909-43-9

Written by Megan Rios

Other Books in The Book On Series

The Book On Life Unscripted
The Book On Risk Management in Payments
The Book On AI for Everyday People
The Book On Relationships
The Book On Master The Algorithm
The Book On Saying No
The Book On Community-Led Strategy
The Book On The Myth of Multitasking
The Book On The Burnout Blueprint
The Book On The Digital Reboot
The Book On The Shape of What's Coming
The Book On Strategic Obsession
The Book On High-Stakes Thinking
The Book On Artificial Leverage
The Book On Clarity
The Book On Uncertainty
The Book On Operational Excellence
The Book On Escape
The Book On Reinvention After Consequences
The Book On Re-Unifying Society
The Book On Taking Flight
The Book On Persuasion
The Book On Enough
The Book On Attention
The Book On Men (for Women)
The Book On Women (for Men)

Table of Contents

CHAPTER 1: UNDERSTANDING THE MALE MIND:............6

THE INSTRUMENTAL MINDSET AND ITS LIMITATIONS 8
THE PERFORMANCE OF MASCULINITY AND ITS HIDDEN COSTS 10
DISCONNECTION AS DEFAULT AND THE CAPACITY FOR CHANGE..... 14

CHAPTER 2: THE EVOLUTION OF MASCULINITY: 17

THE COLLAPSE OF INDUSTRIAL MASCULINITY 18
THE SHAME ECONOMY OF MODERN MANHOOD............................... 21
THE BACKLASH AND THE ALGORITHM 23

CHAPTER 3: EMOTIONAL LITERACY: 29

THE NEUROLOGICAL ARCHITECTURE OF EMOTIONAL PROCESSING 30
THE VOCABULARY GAP AND ITS RELATIONAL CONSEQUENCES........ 32
THE SHAME BARRIER TO LEARNING 35
THE MISSING INFRASTRUCTURE 37

CHAPTER 4: THE FEAR OF VULNERABILITY: 41

THE SOCIAL GEOMETRY OF MALE SELF-DISCLOSURE 42
VULNERABILITY HIERARCHIES AND SELECTIVE DISCLOSURE............. 45
THE WITNESSING PROBLEM AND RESPONSE SCRIPTS 47
COMPARATIVE VULNERABILITY AND THE ZERO-SUM ERROR............ 49
VULNERABILITY TIMING AND THE CRISIS PARADOX 51

CHAPTER 5: COMMUNICATION BREAKDOWN: 54

THE MEANING-MAKING DIVIDE 54
EGO DEFENSE THROUGH INFORMATION CONTROL...................... 57
THE SUBTEXT BLINDNESS PROBLEM 60
THE META-COMMUNICATION FAILURE 62
THE PERFORMANCE OF COMMUNICATION 64
THE LANGUAGE OF REPAIR AND THE APOLOGY IMPASSE................. 67

CHAPTER 6: THE PARADOX OF CONNECTION: 70

THE DEVELOPMENTAL ORIGINS OF AMBIVALENT ATTACHMENT 71
THE ENGULFMENT TERROR AND MASCULINITY MAINTENANCE....... 73
THE CYCLICAL PATTERN OF PURSUIT AND WITHDRAWAL.................. 75
THE COUNTERDEPENDENCE MASQUERADE.......................... 77
THE DISORGANIZED ATTACHMENT LEGACY.......................... 79
THE RECLAMATION OF INTERDEPENDENCE.......................... 81

CHAPTER 7: REDEFINING STRENGTH: 84

THE NEUROCHEMISTRY OF DOMINANCE VERSUS AUTHORITY 86

RESPECT AS MUTUAL RECOGNITION 88

THE ECONOMIC ROOTS OF CONTROL 90

BUILDING RESPECT THROUGH COMPETENCE AND CONSISTENCY 92

CHAPTER 8: THE ROLE OF SOCIETY: 97

THE WORKPLACE AS MASCULINITY TESTING GROUND 98

DIGITAL SURVEILLANCE AND PERFORMANCE METRICS 101

ECONOMIC PRECARITY AND MASCULINE WORTH 104

THE PHYSICAL BODY AS MASCULINE CURRENCY 106

CHAPTER 9: THE JOURNEY TO AUTHENTICITY: 111

THE AUTHENTICITY TAX AND PRIVILEGE INTERSECTIONS 112

THE DISINTEGRATION PHASE AND IDENTITY DISSOLUTION 115

PROVISIONAL IDENTITY AND ITERATIVE BECOMING 118

THE SOCIAL COST OF NON-COMPLIANCE 121

CHAPTER 10: BRIDGING THE GAP: 124

STRATEGIC EMPATHY AND THE OBSERVATIONAL STANCE 125

PRECISION LANGUAGE AND MASCULINE TRANSLATION 128

GRADUATED DISCLOSURE AND THE TRUST LADDER 131

REPAIR PROTOCOLS AND THE RUPTURE-RECOVERY CYCLE 134

Chapter 1: Understanding the Male Mind: Beyond Stereotypes

The contemporary man exists within a profound paradox, one that becomes immediately apparent when we observe the dissonance between what men do and what they need. A successful executive leaves work after closing a major deal, stops by a bar for several drinks with colleagues he barely knows, then returns home to a partner asking about his day, only to offer nothing beyond "fine" and "tired." This is not emotional withholding in the conventional sense. This is something far more complex: a man who genuinely cannot access or articulate the interior landscape of his own experience. The questions women ask, "What are you feeling?" "What do you need?" "What's really going on?", is not being deflected out of stubbornness or manipulation. They are genuinely unanswerable because most men have never been taught the vocabulary, the introspective tools, or the permission to explore those territories within themselves. The male mind operates from a fundamentally different developmental blueprint, one that prioritizes external performance over internal awareness, action over reflection, and stoicism over emotional literacy. Understanding this distinction is not about excusing problematic behavior or lowering standards for emotional engagement. Rather, it provides the necessary framework for recognizing that when men appear emotionally unavailable, they often are, even to themselves.

The architecture of male psychology begins its construction long before most people recognize that its foundation is being laid. By age three, boys have already absorbed the implicit lessons that emotional expression beyond anger carries social penalties. Research in developmental psychology reveals that parents. Chapter 6: The Paradox of Connection: Craving Yet Resist. When Developmental Origins of Ambivalent Attachment   27 narrows dramatically to a handful of acceptable states: happy, angry, tired, fine. This linguistic deprivation creates what scholars call "normative male alexithymia", a culturally induced inability to identify and describe emotional states that affects the majority of men to varying degrees. By elementary school, boys learn that tears invite mockery, that fear must be concealed, that admitting pain makes them targets. The peer enforcement of these rules is ruthless and relentless. A boy who cries on the playground discovers immediately that his social currency has plummeted. He learns that vulnerability is not a pathway to connection but a liability that invites exploitation. These early experiences do not simply teach boys to hide emotions; they fundamentally alter the neural pathways associated with emotional processing. Repeated suppression of vulnerable feelings creates a pattern where accessing those emotions becomes genuinely difficult, not merely socially uncomfortable. The neural connections that would ordinarily facilitate emotional awareness atrophy from disuse while pathways associated with performance, competition, and instrumental thinking strengthen. This is not a metaphor. Brain imaging studies demonstrate measurable differences in how men and women process emotional information, with men showing reduced activity in regions associated with emotional labeling and increased activity in areas tied to problem-solving and action planning when confronted with emotional stimuli.

The Instrumental Mindset and Its Limitations

What women often interpret as emotional coldness or dismissiveness in men frequently stems from what psychologists identify as an "instrumental orientation", a cognitive framework that automatically converts emotional situations into problems requiring solutions rather than experiences requiring acknowledgment. When a woman shares a difficult experience from her day, she is typically seeking emotional resonance, validation, and connection. The male mind, however, has been trained since childhood to respond to distress by immediately scanning for actionable solutions. This is not callousness; it is the automatic operation of a mental framework that equates caring with fixing. The frustration women experience when men respond to emotional sharing with advice rather than empathy reflects a genuine communication failure. Still, one is rooted in fundamentally different understandings of what caring looks like. For most men, offering solutions is how they demonstrate love and concern. It represents their attempt to reduce the other person's suffering through practical intervention. The concept that simply witnessing and acknowledging pain might itself be valuable feels foreign, even counterproductive, to the instrumental mindset. This framework served important evolutionary and social functions historically, enabling men to compartmentalize fear during dangerous tasks, to focus on threat assessment and resource acquisition without being overwhelmed by emotion, and to maintain group cohesion through shared activity rather than emotional intimacy. However, these same adaptive strategies become maladaptive in the context of intimate relationships that require sustained emotional attunement and vulnerability.

The instrumental orientation reveals itself in countless daily interactions that women find baffling or hurtful. A man returns from a doctor's appointment that revealed concerning health results and responds to his partner's worried inquiries with logistical details about follow-up appointments and treatment options while entirely bypassing his own fear or anxiety about the diagnosis. When pressed about his feelings, he becomes irritated or withdrawn, not because he is hiding something he knows, but because the question itself feels unanswerable and accusatory. His mind has automatically moved to the management phase, scheduling tests, researching options, developing an action plan, because this feels like forward movement, like taking control of a threatening situation. The idea of pausing to sit with fear, to name it, to share it, strikes him as counterproductive, as dwelling unnecessarily in discomfort when action is possible. This pattern intensifies during relationship conflicts. When a woman expresses dissatisfaction with some aspect of their connection, many men immediately experience this as a problem they have failed to solve, which triggers shame and defensive reactions. The man's mind races to identify what specific actions would resolve the issue, while his partner is seeking something entirely different: to be heard, understood, and emotionally met. The result is a conversation where both people are speaking different languages, each feeling increasingly frustrated that the other cannot grasp what seems obvious from their own perspective.

What further complicates the male psychological landscape is the profound shame that surrounds any perceived failure, particularly failures related to providing, protecting, or performing. Male identity construction relies heavily on competence and capability, creating a psychological vulnerability around any situation that exposes limitations or inadequacies. This shame operates below conscious awareness for most men, manifesting as irritation, withdrawal, or deflection rather than being recognized and named as shame itself. When a man cannot solve a problem his partner brings to him, when he struggles financially, when he fails to satisfy sexually, when he cannot fix her unhappiness, these situations trigger deep identity threats that most men lack the framework to process productively. The typical male response is to either double down on instrumental action (trying harder to fix the problem) or withdraw from the situation entirely to protect against the overwhelming sense of inadequacy. Neither response addresses the underlying emotional reality or creates the conditions for genuine intimacy. The tragedy is that this shame-driven pattern prevents men from accessing the very connection that might ease their distress. Admitting struggle, acknowledging limitation, and asking for help require a level of vulnerability that conflicts with deeply internalized messages about what it means to be a man. The result is a self-reinforcing cycle where emotional isolation intensifies shame, which further prevents the vulnerability needed to break the isolation.

The Performance of Masculinity and Its Hidden Costs

Perhaps no aspect of male psychology is more misunderstood than the constant, exhausting performance of masculinity itself. For most men, gender is not something they are; it is something they do, continuously and anxiously. Masculinity operates as a precarious social status that must be repeatedly proven and can be revoked at any moment through perceived failure. Sociologist

Michael Kimmel describes masculinity as a "relentless test," one that men fail in countless small ways throughout their lives. This performance orientation begins in boyhood and never truly ends, creating a state of chronic vigilance about whether one's behavior, appearance, emotions, and choices measure up to masculine standards. The male mind develops what might be called a "third-person evaluator," an internalized audience constantly assessing whether he appears weak, feminine, incompetent, or otherwise failing at masculinity. This evaluator operates automatically and often unconsciously, influencing everything from posture to emotional expression to career choices to relationship dynamics. When a man appears overly concerned with seeming tough, refusing to admit uncertainty, or avoiding activities deemed feminine, he is often responding to this internal evaluator's harsh judgments. The performance is not necessarily directed at external audiences, though those certainly matter. It is also directed inward, toward maintaining a self-concept of masculine adequacy that feels perpetually under threat.

The energy expenditure required for this constant performance is substantial and largely invisible to those not engaged in it. Every interaction carries the potential for emasculation, every choice risks revealing inadequacy, every moment of vulnerability might expose the supposedly shameful truth that he does not, in fact, have it all together. This vigilance depletes psychological resources that might otherwise be available for introspection, emotional processing, or genuine intimacy. Furthermore, the performance requirement creates an adversarial relationship with one's own authentic experience. If a man feels afraid, overwhelmed, tender, or uncertain, all entirely normal human experiences, those feelings represent failures of the masculine ideal. They must be suppressed, reframed, or converted into anger, which alone among vulnerable emotions retains masculine acceptability. This constant warfare against significant portions of one's own emotional reality is psychologically corrosive. It prevents self-knowledge, distorts decision-making, and fundamentally undermines the possibility of authentic connection. How can a man be truly intimate with another person when he cannot be intimate with himself? How can he offer emotional honesty when he has spent decades systematically lying to himself about his own inner experience? The performance of masculinity creates men who are strangers to themselves, and this self-alienation inevitably manifests as emotional unavailability in relationships.

The masculine performance imperative also explains why many men react with defensiveness or hostility when their partner expresses dissatisfaction or requests change. Such feedback represents not merely a disagreement about behavior but a fundamental threat to masculine adequacy. If he were a real man, a good man, a competent man, the feedback suggests, he would already be doing what is being requested. The request itself, therefore, functions as evidence of his failure. This interpretation, though rarely conscious or articulated, triggers intense defensive reactions designed to protect against the shame of inadequacy. The man may counterattack by pointing out his partner's flaws, minimizing the validity of her concerns, or withdrawing emotionally as a way of refusing to engage with threatening feedback. These defensive maneuvers are not calculated manipulation, though they can certainly be destructive. They are automatic protective responses from a psyche organized around avoiding the experience of masculine failure. What women often perceive as ego or stubbornness is frequently unprocessed shame manifesting as defensiveness. Understanding this dynamic does not require accepting these defensive reactions or accommodating them. However, it does reframe them from intentional cruelty or indifference to reflexive psychological self-protection, which opens different possibilities for addressing the pattern.

The competitive framework that dominates male social development further shapes the male mind in ways that complicate intimate relationships. From early childhood, boys learn to navigate social hierarchies where one's position is constantly negotiated through competition, dominance displays, and careful attention to relative status. Male friendships, while often deeply meaningful, typically develop through shared activity rather than emotional disclosure. Men bond by doing things together, playing sports, working on projects, pursuing common interests, rather than through the face-to-face emotional intimacy that characterizes many female friendships. This creates a particular kind of connection that feels genuine and important but does not develop the skills required for intimate partnership. The typical man enters romantic relationships having had very few experiences of sustained emotional vulnerability with another person. He may have close male friends but has likely never discussed his deepest fears, insecurities, or emotional needs with them. The relationship context, therefore, demands capacities he has rarely, if ever, practiced. Furthermore, the competitive framework that structures male relationships creates an adversarial undertone that can infiltrate romantic partnerships. When disagreements arise, some men unconsciously frame them as competitions to be won rather than problems to be collaboratively resolved. The goal becomes proving oneself right rather than understanding the other's perspective or finding mutually satisfactory solutions. This competitive orientation directly conflicts with the collaboration and mutual vulnerability required for healthy intimate relationships.

Disconnection as Default and the Capacity for Change

The cumulative effect of these developmental and social forces is that emotional disconnection becomes the default mode for many men. It is not that men lack the capacity for emotional depth, introspection, or intimate connection. Rather, they typically lack practice in accessing these capacities and face substantial internal and external barriers to developing them. The male mind has been systematically trained away from emotional literacy for decades by the time most men enter serious adult relationships. The resulting emotional unavailability is not a character flaw or a choice in any meaningful sense. It is the predictable outcome of a socialization process that prioritized other capabilities while actively punishing emotional development. This distinction matters enormously for how we understand male behavior in relationships. When a man struggles to articulate his feelings, cannot identify what he needs emotionally, or withdraws when conversations become vulnerable, he is typically not being intentionally withholding or manipulative. He is operating at the limits of his developed capacities. This is simultaneously an explanation and not an excuse. Understanding the origins of emotional limitations does not require accepting them as immutable or lowering expectations for emotional engagement in relationships. However, it does suggest that change requires more than simply demanding different behavior. It requires recognizing that many men need to develop entirely new capabilities, learning to identify emotions, tolerate vulnerability, communicate inner experience, that were never part of their developmental curriculum.

The important and hopeful reality is that the male mind retains plasticity throughout life. The neural pathways that atrophied during boyhood can be strengthened through practice and intention. Men can develop emotional literacy, though it requires sustained effort and often feels deeply uncomfortable initially. The process resembles learning a new language as an adult, possible but requiring patience, practice, and accepting that initial attempts will be clumsy and frustrating. Men who successfully develop greater emotional awareness consistently report that the initial work felt awkward, even threatening, but that persisting through that discomfort eventually opened access to richer inner experience and more satisfying relationships. However, this development rarely happens spontaneously. It requires both internal motivation and external support. A man must want to develop these capacities for his own reasons, not merely to satisfy a partner's demands. Attempting to change only to avoid conflict or prevent relationship loss typically fails because the internal motivation is insufficient to sustain effort through the discomfort of growth. Additionally, men benefit enormously from environments where vulnerability is modeled and normalized, whether through therapy, men's groups, or friendships where emotional honesty is practiced. Isolation reinforces the patterns established in boyhood, while a community that values emotional authenticity creates conditions where different ways of being become possible.

Understanding the male mind beyond stereotypes requires holding multiple truths simultaneously. Men are shaped by forces largely beyond their conscious control, and they retain agency and responsibility for their choices. Men often struggle with emotional capacities through no fault of their own, and they can develop those capacities with intention and support. Men's emotional limitations create genuine pain in relationships, and those limitations are themselves painful for men, whether or not they recognize that pain. The male mind is not defective or inferior; it has been optimized for capabilities that served important functions while neglecting others that prove essential for intimate partnership. This foundation of understanding makes it possible to engage with male psychology not from a place of judgment or resignation but from curiosity and clarity. The chapters that follow will explore specific dimensions of male experience, sexuality, communication, conflict, vulnerability, commitment, with this foundational framework in place. The goal throughout is neither to excuse problematic behavior nor to paint men as hopeless, but to illuminate what is actually happening beneath the surface of behaviors that often confuse, frustrate, or hurt women. With understanding comes the possibility of more effective engagement, clearer boundaries, and realistic expectations. Perhaps most importantly, it creates space to distinguish between men who are genuinely trying to grow beyond their limitations and those who are unwilling to examine themselves, a distinction that matters enormously for women deciding how to invest their emotional energy and where to set their standards for partnership.

Chapter 2: The Evolution of Masculinity: A Crisis in Identity

The modern man navigates existence without a map. His grandfather possessed a clear blueprint for manhood: provide financially, protect physically, project strength, contain emotion, make decisions, lead the family, work until retirement, die with dignity. That blueprint was transmitted through modeling, apprenticeship, and cultural reinforcement. Every institution, workplace, church, military, sports team, echoed the same definitions of masculine success. Today, that unified narrative has shattered into countless fragments, and no coherent replacement has emerged. Men find themselves caught between obsolete ideals they cannot quite abandon and emerging expectations they cannot quite fulfill. This confusion runs deeper than simple role adjustment. It represents a fundamental crisis of identity in which the very essence of what it means to be masculine remains violently contested across every domain of public discourse. The result is a generation of men experiencing what sociologists term "anomie", a profound normlessness in which traditional guides to behavior have collapsed, yet new norms remain ambiguous or contradictory. This is not merely about confusion over who pays for dinner or whether crying is acceptable. This is existential disorientation about the core value of masculine existence itself.

Historical masculinity constructed itself through opposition and scarcity. A boy became a man by proving he was not a woman, not a child, not weak, not emotional, not dependent. Manhood was something achieved through ordeal, validated by other men, and perpetually at risk of revocation. Anthropologist David Gilmore's cross-cultural research documented that across diverse societies, manhood consistently required demonstration through three universal imperatives: impregnating women, protecting dependents, and provisioning for families. These biological and social imperatives created what Gilmore termed "the manhood threshold", a clear demarcation between boyhood and masculine status that demanded public proof. The ordeal might be hunting dangerous game, enduring physical pain without complaint, accumulating wealth, demonstrating sexual prowess, or exhibiting courage in warfare. Regardless of cultural specifics, the pattern remained consistent: manhood was earned through trial, not granted through biology. This framework created enormous psychological pressure but also provided clarity. A man knew what was expected. He understood the criteria for success and failure. He could measure his masculine adequacy against observable standards shared across his community. The system was often brutal and exclusionary, but it was legible.

The Collapse of Industrial Masculinity

The twentieth century cemented a particular form of masculinity around industrial labor and bureaucratic organization. Millions of men defined themselves through their work in factories, construction sites, mining operations, and corporate hierarchies where physical strength, technical expertise, and hierarchical advancement marked masculine achievement. The postwar era in Western societies represented perhaps the apex of this model, when a single male income could support an entire family, when corporate employment offered lifetime security, when manual competence translated directly to economic survival, and when public and private spheres remained rigidly segregated by gender. This was the masculinity of the "organization man" and the blue-collar worker alike, defined by productive capacity, measured by paycheck size, validated by dependents successfully supported. Emotional life remained peripheral, relegated to women's domain. A man's interior world was largely irrelevant to his social value, which derived almost entirely from what he could do, build, earn, or protect. The psychological costs were immense, but the social benefits seemed clear: men received status, authority, and identity in exchange for their labor and emotional suppression.

This entire structure has undergone catastrophic destabilization over the past forty years. Deindustrialization eliminated millions of manufacturing jobs that once provided working-class men with both income and identity. Globalization and automation continue eroding traditional male-dominated sectors while expanding service and care work historically coded as feminine. The gender wage gap, though persistent, has narrowed significantly, and women now earn the majority of college degrees, transforming educational hierarchies that once favored men. Legal and cultural changes have dismantled institutional male privileges across domains from family law to workplace policy to reproductive autonomy. Marriage rates have declined, cohabitation has increased, and women initiate the majority of divorces, signaling shifts in relationship power dynamics. Meanwhile, the rise of digital technology has transformed work itself, privileging cognitive and emotional labor over physical strength, collaborative skills over command authority, and flexibility over rigid role adherence. For men raised with expectations shaped by previous generations, these transformations feel less like progress and more like the ground disappearing beneath their feet. What happens to masculine identity when its traditional anchors, breadwinning, physical prowess, institutional authority, guaranteed deference, no longer function as reliable sources of status or self-worth?

The crisis intensifies because no clear alternative narrative has achieved cultural consensus. Various competing masculinities now vie for legitimacy, each claiming authenticity while condemning others as inadequate or toxic. Traditional masculinity persists in certain subcultures, reasserting old hierarchies and resisting change as degradation. Progressive masculinity attempts to construct male identity around feminist principles, emotional openness, and egalitarian relationships, but often struggles with the tension between male particularity and feminist criticism of masculine-coded traits. Therapeutic masculinity encourages men to process feelings and seek help, yet remains vulnerable to accusations of narcissism or weakness. Entrepreneurial masculinity celebrates hustle culture and self-optimization, offering achievement without traditional employment structures, but often repackages old competitive imperatives in a new language. Online communities promote various forms of hypermasculinity, teaching men to maximize sexual success, financial gain, or physical dominance through calculated strategies that treat relationships as zero-sum competitions. Each model offers partial solutions while generating new problems and contradictions. The proliferation of options itself becomes paralyzing: men are told to be strong but sensitive, successful but humble, confident but respectful, assertive but egalitarian, independent but connected. These demands are not simply challenging, they are frequently mutually contradictory, requiring men to perform impossible simultaneous states of being.

The Shame Economy of Modern Manhood

Contemporary masculine identity operates within what might be termed a "shame economy", a system in which virtually every possible masculine expression attracts condemnation from some quarter. Express traditional masculine traits, and face accusations of toxicity, patriarchal violence, or outdated thinking. Reject traditional masculinity entirely, and endure mockery as weak, emasculated, or performatively woke. Succeed economically, and be dismissed as privileged and unaware. Fail economically, and be judged as inadequate to basic masculine responsibilities. Remain stoic, and be criticized as emotionally stunted, express vulnerability, and risk being perceived as unattractive or burdensome. Take leadership, and face suspicion of dominance and control. Step back, and encounter disappointment about passivity or lack of initiative. Attempt to discuss male-specific issues, and be accused of derailing important conversations about female oppression. Stay silent, and be condemned for complicity in systems of male power. This is not hyperbole, these are experienced realities reported consistently by men across therapeutic contexts, support groups, and research interviews about contemporary masculine experience.

The shame economy creates what researchers describe as "precarious manhood", the pervasive sense that masculine status remains perpetually unstable and subject to instant revocation through insufficient performance or inadequate adherence to ever-shifting standards. Unlike femininity, which most cultures treat as a biological given that might be performed well or poorly but cannot be fundamentally lost, masculinity in most societies functions as a conditional social status that requires ongoing validation and defense against constant threats of degradation. Psychologists Jennifer Bosson and Joseph Vandello have conducted extensive research demonstrating that across cultures, manhood is understood as more tenuous than womanhood, more easily lost through failure or shame, and more dependent on public demonstration rather than private conviction. Their experimental studies reveal that when masculine status is threatened, through failure at traditionally masculine tasks, through comparison to women who outperform them, or through assignment of feminine-coded activities, men show significant increases in anxiety, aggressive behavior, and compensatory masculine displays. This is not a conscious calculation but a visceral threat response, suggesting that masculine identity threat activates primitive defensive systems rather than rational assessment.

The contemporary shame economy amplifies this precariousness exponentially by multiplying the criteria for masculine failure while simultaneously making those criteria contradictory and unstable. A man can no longer secure masculine status by mastering a single domain, say, economic provision or physical strength, because other domains now carry equal or greater weight in determining masculine adequacy. He must simultaneously demonstrate economic competence, emotional intelligence, physical fitness, sexual prowess, egalitarian values, authentic vulnerability, confident leadership, respectful deference, ambitious drive, and spiritual depth. These expectations arrive from multiple sources: romantic partners, workplace cultures, peer groups, family members, therapeutic discourse, political movements, and algorithmic media environments that reward engagement through moral outrage and social comparison. The standards constantly shift based on context, audience, and current discourse trends. What counts as appropriately masculine behavior in one setting becomes problematic in another. What demonstrates evolved masculinity to one person signals weakness or performance to another. Men report feeling perpetually off-balance, unable to establish stable ground for identity construction, constantly adjusting and second-guessing their expressions against an incomprehensible matrix of competing demands.

The Backlash and the Algorithm

This identity chaos has made men extraordinarily vulnerable to movements and ideologies offering clear answers and masculine validation. The past decade has witnessed explosive growth in online communities dedicated to teaching men strategies for success in dating, career advancement, physical development, and life optimization. Some of these spaces provide genuinely useful information about fitness, professional development, or social skills. Others have metastasized into toxic subcultures promoting misogyny, conspiracy theories, and political radicalization. The common thread connecting them is clarity, they provide men with explicit masculine frameworks in an environment of overwhelming ambiguity. The promise is seductive: follow these principles, complete these tasks, adopt this mindset, and you will achieve masculine adequacy that society otherwise denies you. You will understand what women really want despite what they say. You will protect yourself from exploitation and manipulation. You will reclaim the power that contemporary culture has stripped from men. You will escape the shame economy by rejecting its legitimacy entirely.

These communities understand something crucial that mainstream discourse often misses: men are desperate for guidance, and the traditional institutions that once provided masculine mentorship have largely collapsed or been discredited. Fathers are usually absent or emotionally unavailable, themselves struggling with their own masculine confusion. Male friendship groups have become increasingly rare as men report fewer close friends and less intimate conversation than previous generations. Religious institutions have declined in influence and membership. Youth organizations like scouts or athletic leagues face constant criticism and reduced participation. Educational environments from elementary school through university have become increasingly female-dominated in both enrollment and staffing. Mental health services remain underutilized by men due to stigma and therapeutic approaches often designed around female communication patterns. The vacuum created by these institutional declines has been filled by algorithmic content delivery systems that excel at identifying confusion and monetizing solutions. A young man searches online for information about approaching women or building confidence, and the algorithm detects engagement with that content, then progressively delivers more extreme material that promises ever more comprehensive answers while fostering dependence on the content creator and community. The path from "how to talk to women" to consuming content about sexual market value, hypergamy theories, and evolutionary psychology explanations for why women are fundamentally different and often deceptive can be traversed in weeks of algorithmic progression.

The brilliance and danger of these digital spaces lie in their sophisticated understanding of masculine psychology. They provide exactly what men experiencing identity confusion crave: a comprehensive explanatory framework, a clear hierarchy of values and goals, a community of similar others, concrete action steps, measurable progress metrics, and validation of grievances that mainstream discourse dismisses. They operate through a mixture of legitimate observations (the job market has changed, traditional relationship scripts are confused, men face genuine challenges), emotional exploitation (fostering resentment and victimization), and ideological capture (directing justified frustration toward reactionary political conclusions and interpersonal strategies). The emotional hook is profound: these communities tell men that their confusion and pain are not personal failings but rational responses to systemic anti-male bias. They transform shame into righteous anger. They convert isolation into belonging. They replace uncertainty with certainty. For a man drowning in identity confusion and starving for masculine validation, these spaces can feel like lifelines, even as they often lead toward greater isolation, bitterness, and inability to form genuine intimate connections.

Understanding this phenomenon requires recognizing that radicalization is not a problem of individual moral failure but a predictable outcome of identity crisis meeting sophisticated exploitation. When legitimate developmental needs go unmet, the need for mentorship, belonging, purpose, and coherent identity, humans become vulnerable to movements that promise to fulfill those needs, regardless of whether those movements ultimately deliver on their promises or lead toward destructive outcomes. The young man who falls into extremist online spaces is not fundamentally different from the young man who finds healthy community through sports, church, or professional mentorship. Both are seeking the same things: clarity about how to be a man, validation that their masculinity has value, connection with others who understand their experience, and guidance for navigating a world that feels increasingly hostile and confusing. The difference lies not in the needs themselves but in which institutional structures capture that seeking energy and direct it toward constructive or destructive ends. Contemporary society has largely failed to construct healthy, widely accessible institutions for masculine identity formation that can compete with the emotional intensity, comprehensive narratives, and immediate accessibility of digital radicalization pipelines.

The challenge for women seeking to understand men is recognizing that the masculine identity crisis is not theoretical or exaggerated, it represents lived psychological reality for millions of men navigating contemporary existence. This crisis does not excuse harmful behavior, misogyny, or emotional abdication. However, understanding the situation is essential for interpreting male behavior that otherwise appears inexplicable or intentionally hurtful. The man who becomes defensive when discussing gender issues may not be willfully ignorant but is experiencing the conversation as an attack on an already unstable identity. The man who retreats into work, gaming, or substance use may be seeking refuge from an identity confusion that creates constant background anxiety. The man who clings to outdated masculine performances may not be ideologically committed to patriarchy but terrified of free-falling in a world where he cannot identify what counts as valuable masculine existence. The man who becomes angry or withdrawn when relationship expectations shift may not be punishing his partner but drowning in demands he cannot fulfill while maintaining coherent selfhood. These realities do not make such behavior acceptable. Still, they transform it from a malicious choice into a desperate coping, a distinction that matters profoundly for determining appropriate responses and realistic expectations.

The evolution of masculinity represents an ongoing rupture without resolution, a collapse of old certainties that has not yet produced stable new formations. Men inhabit this rupture differently based on generation, class, race, education, and individual psychology, but the underlying dynamics touch nearly all men in contemporary Western societies. The question is not whether this evolution will continue, it will, because the economic and cultural transformations driving it remain in motion. The question is whether society will construct healthy pathways through this identity crisis or whether men will continue navigating it through isolation, compensation, addiction, radicalization, and relationship failure. For women, understanding this crisis means recognizing that much of what appears as masculine pathology or relational failure actually represents disoriented attempts to construct identity in the absence of reliable guides. The men and women encountered today are not defective versions of their grandfathers, they are fundamentally different creatures facing fundamentally different challenges, often without the psychological or cultural resources necessary to meet those challenges successfully. That understanding changes nothing about what women deserve in relationships. Still, it changes everything about how to interpret what they actually encounter and whether bridges across this gender confusion remain possible.

Chapter 3: Emotional Literacy: The Silent Struggle

The average man possesses approximately 15,000 words of emotional vocabulary theoretically available to him in the English language. Yet when asked to describe his internal experience, he defaults to perhaps five: fine, good, tired, stressed, and angry. This reduction reveals something far more troubling than mere laziness or disinterest. It exposes a profound disability that most men do not recognize they possess, and many women fail to understand as genuine incapacity rather than willful withholding. Emotional literacy, the ability to identify, understand, articulate, and modulate one's own emotional states, develops through explicit teaching and practice, neither of which most boys receive. While girls spend their developmental years engaged in elaborate emotional rehearsals through conversational play, narrative sharing, and relational processing, boys inhabit a parallel universe where emotional experience gets translated into physical action, competitive ranking, or simply ignored until it disappears. The consequence is not that men lack emotions, but that they lack the fundamental cognitive and linguistic architecture to process them. This creates a peculiar form of internal blindness in which a man experiences powerful physiological and psychological reactions but cannot name them, cannot understand their origins, and therefore cannot communicate them to others or regulate them effectively. The result resembles trying to navigate complex terrain without a map or vocabulary to describe landmarks, rendering even the most motivated man functionally mute when confronted with the question of what he feels.

The Neurological Architecture of Emotional Processing

Recent neuroscience research utilizing functional magnetic resonance imaging has revealed striking differences in how male and female brains process emotional information, though the critical finding is that these differences are substantially learned rather than innate. Studies conducted by Dr. Lisa Feldman Barrett at Northeastern University demonstrate that emotional recognition and categorization require repeated practice to develop the neural pathways linking physiological sensations to conceptual categories. Women typically receive thousands more hours of this practice during childhood and adolescence, creating more elaborate neural networks for emotional processing. When women experience physiological arousal, increased heart rate, muscle tension, stomach tightness, their brains automatically scan a rich conceptual landscape to categorize the experience: Is this anxiety about an upcoming conversation? Resentment about an unresolved conflict? Excitement mixed with nervousness about a new opportunity? The brain constructs emotional experience by matching physical sensations to learned categories, and women possess more categories, more nuanced distinctions, and more practiced pathways for making these matches. Men's brains, by contrast, often register the physical sensation without successfully categorizing it, resulting in a vague sense of discomfort or activation without a meaningful emotional label attached. This is not emotional suppression, the man is not hiding anger and calling it "fine." He genuinely experiences a diffuse, unlabeled physiological state that his brain cannot successfully categorize into a useful emotional concept.

This neurological reality explains patterns that women frequently interpret as evasion or manipulation. A man becomes visibly tense during a conversation about his mother's declining health, his shoulders hunched, his jaw clenched, his responses terse and defensive. Asked what he is feeling, he responds with genuine confusion: "Nothing, I'm fine." He is not lying. His body is exhibiting a clear stress response, but his brain has not successfully constructed an emotional experience from these sensations. He lacks the practiced neural architecture to recognize this particular constellation of physical symptoms as grief, or fear of loss, or helpless frustration about his inability to prevent her deterioration, or guilt about not visiting more frequently. His emotional construction system has failed, leaving him with bodily discomfort he wants to escape rather than a named feeling he can explore or share. When pressed, he becomes irritated not because he is protecting a secret, but because the questioning itself intensifies his discomfort without providing any path toward resolution. The woman's insistence that he must be feeling something strikes him as accusatory rather than helpful, she is demanding he produce something he does not have access to, like asking someone to describe a color they cannot see. The tragedy is that the feeling exists in his body, affecting his behavior and his stress levels, but it remains neurologically invisible to his conscious awareness.

The construction of emotional experience requires not only recognition but also narrative coherence, the ability to tell a story about why a feeling makes sense given circumstances and history. Women typically develop elaborate causal narratives about their emotional states through years of conversational processing with other women. A woman might explain: "I felt anxious about the party because last time we went to one of his work events, I felt excluded from conversations and he did not notice I was struggling, which reminded me of feeling invisible in my family growing up." This narrative weaves together current context, experience, and relational dynamics into a coherent emotional story. Men rarely develop this skill. Their emotional narratives, when they exist at all, tend to be sparse and situation-focused: "The traffic made me angry." The poverty of these narratives is not evidence of shallow feeling but of underdeveloped narrative skills. Without practice in constructing emotional stories, men cannot understand their own reactions as meaningful patterns connected to deeper needs and histories. This leaves them perpetually confused by their own responses, unable to predict what will trigger strong reactions or to explain their behavior to partners who reasonably expect some accounting for sudden withdrawal, irritation, or coldness.

The Vocabulary Gap and Its Relational Consequences

Linguistic research on emotional vocabulary reveals that the average woman actively uses approximately three times as many distinct emotion words as the average man in everyday conversation. More significant than raw numbers is the sophistication of emotional distinctions. While a man might use "angry" as an umbrella term for a vast range of experiences, a woman distinguishes between frustrated, resentful, irritated, bitter, furious, livid, indignant, and dozens of other variants that capture meaningful differences in intensity, attribution, and action tendency. These are not pretentious distinctions. Each word captures a genuinely different subjective experience and implies different needs and appropriate responses. Feeling frustrated suggests obstacle-removal would help; feeling resentful suggests past boundary violations need addressing; feeling indignant suggests injustice requires confrontation. When a man collapses all of these into "angry," he loses access to crucial information about what he actually needs and what would genuinely help resolve the feeling. This vocabulary poverty creates particular problems in intimate relationships where emotional precision is essential for repair and resolution. A woman needs to know whether her partner is disappointed in her specifically or simply discouraged about life circumstances, whether he is anxious about their relationship or experiencing free-floating worry, whether he is hurt by something she said or carrying unresolved pain from his past that her words triggered. Without vocabulary for these distinctions, men provide impossibly vague information that leaves their partners guessing and often guessing wrong.

The consequences of this vocabulary gap extend beyond communication problems into the realm of emotional regulation. Research in affective science demonstrates that the ability to make fine-grained distinctions between emotional states, called "emotional granularity", predicts better emotion regulation outcomes. When someone can identify that they are experiencing "melancholy" rather than generic "sadness," or "apprehensive" rather than generic "anxious," they gain useful information about appropriate coping strategies and the likely duration and trajectory of the feeling. Men's poverty of emotional vocabulary limits their regulatory capacity, leaving them with blunt instruments when fine tools are required. Unable to distinguish between different varieties of distress, many men default to the same crude responses regardless of the actual emotional need: withdrawal, distraction through work or substances, physical activity, or explosion into anger that at least feels like taking action. These strategies sometimes work, often fail, and rarely represent an optimal match for the underlying emotional state. The man himself cannot articulate why, sometimes, going for a run helps and sometimes it does not, why some days he can tolerate relationship tension and other days he needs to escape the house. He lacks the internal information that would allow him to match regulatory strategy to emotional need because he cannot accurately identify what the need is.

Women frequently interpret this vocabulary poverty as evidence that men either do not experience emotions intensely or are choosing not to share their emotional lives. Both interpretations fundamentally misunderstand the situation. Men experience emotions with equal or sometimes greater physiological intensity than women, their heart rates spike as high, their cortisol levels surge as dramatically, their bodies register threat and loss just as powerfully. The difference lies entirely in their ability to translate this physiological experience into articulable, shareable, psychologically meaningful content. A man's body is screaming with anxiety before an important presentation. Still, when his partner asks how he is feeling, he genuinely has access only to "I'm fine, just thinking about work." His body knows, but his mind cannot construct the experience into something nameable and communicable. This is why men's emotional experience often seems to emerge as physical symptoms rather than psychological ones, the unnamed anxiety becomes insomnia, headaches, digestive problems, and muscle tension that the man experiences as purely physical maladies requiring physical solutions. The emotional content remains inaccessible to consciousness, expressing itself only through the body's distress signals that the mind cannot interpret correctly.

The Shame Barrier to Learning

Perhaps the most devastating aspect of male emotional illiteracy is that it carries enormous shame, which creates a vicious cycle preventing remedy. Boys learn early that emotional incompetence marks them as insufficiently masculine. The boy who cries easily, who talks about feelings, who needs comfort, faces social punishment from peers and often subtle or explicit disappointment from adults. By adolescence, most boys have internalized the message that emotional literacy is feminine and that possessing it would compromise their masculine standing. This creates a profound bind: the very skill they need to navigate relationships and psychological well-being is the skill they have learned to reject as incompatible with their gender identity. Adult men carry this shame into their intimate relationships, where their emotional illiteracy becomes obvious and problematic, but feels too humiliating to acknowledge directly. When a woman expresses frustration with his inability to discuss feelings, a man experiences this as an attack on his fundamental adequacy as a person. He cannot simply admit "I do not know how to do this" because that admission feels like confessing to catastrophic failure. Instead, he defends, deflects, or attacks back, insisting that his partner is too emotional, too demanding, too focused on talking instead of doing.

This defensive stance prevents the learning that could resolve the problem. Emotional literacy can be learned at any age, but it requires the vulnerable admission that one currently lacks the skill, followed by patient practice under conditions of safety rather than criticism. Most intimate relationships cannot provide these conditions because the stakes are too high and the woman's frustration too intense. She needs him to be emotionally literate now, for the relationship to function, and her pressure for immediate competence makes the learning environment feel dangerous rather than safe. The man experiences her requests for emotional sharing as demands he cannot meet, which intensifies his shame and his defensive withdrawal. She interprets his withdrawal as a refusal rather than an incapacity, which intensifies her frustration and her demands. The cycle accelerates until emotional conversation becomes a battlefield where both parties feel attacked and neither feels understood. Breaking this cycle requires recognizing emotional illiteracy as a genuine developmental deficit rather than a character flaw or a choice, which means approaching it with the patience and structured teaching one would apply to any complex skill being learned from scratch by an adult who missed critical developmental windows.

The comparison to learning a second language in adulthood proves instructive. An adult learning French does not magically acquire fluency through sheer willpower or through being yelled at for not being fluent. They require structured instruction, vocabulary building, grammar lessons, patient correction, and extensive practice in low-stakes environments before they can function in high-stakes conversations. They will make countless errors, experience profound frustration, and need encouragement rather than criticism to persist through the difficult middle stages where they understand their inadequacy acutely but have not yet developed real competence. Emotional literacy requires exactly this kind of developmental patience, yet intimate relationships rarely provide it. Instead, couples attempt to have crucial emotional conversations in the target language before the man has learned basic vocabulary, then interpret his failure as evidence of bad faith rather than genuine inability. The woman's legitimate need for emotional connection collides with the man's legitimate lack of capacity, creating a seemingly irresolvable standoff that both experience as the other's fault.

The Missing Infrastructure of Male Emotional Development

The larger social context fails to provide men with the infrastructure necessary for developing emotional literacy outside of intimate relationships, leaving romantic partners to bear the entire burden of teaching these skills. Women typically maintain multiple emotionally intimate friendships throughout their lives where they practice emotional articulation, receive validation and feedback, and develop their emotional vocabulary through constant use. These friendships function as crucial sites of emotional skill-building and regulation, providing safe contexts for trying out emotional narratives, testing interpretations of complex feelings, and receiving help with emotional categorization when one's own understanding fails. Men rarely possess equivalent relationships. Research by sociologists studying male friendship patterns finds that most men beyond their twenties lack any friendship involving regular emotional disclosure or psychological vulnerability. Their friendships center on shared activities, humor, and practical support, all of which have value but none of which build emotional literacy. When emotional content does emerge, it typically gets deflected quickly through jokes or advice-giving rather than explored in depth. This means men enter intimate relationships with romantic partners as their only source of emotional skill-building, placing impossible pressure on that single relationship to provide what should be supported by an entire network of emotionally intimate connections.

The absence of this infrastructure creates several destructive patterns. First, men develop emotional dependence on their romantic partners that feels suffocating to women while remaining largely invisible to the men themselves. Because the partner is his only source of emotional processing and regulation, her unavailability creates a genuine crisis for him, even though he cannot articulate this need or even recognize it consciously. He experiences her time with friends, her need for space, and her separate interests as threatening to his emotional survival because she has become his sole emotional lifeline. This dependence creates controlling behavior that appears to be about possession or insecurity but is actually about unrecognized emotional need. Second, when the relationship ends, men often suffer catastrophic emotional deregulation because they have lost their only site for emotional processing while simultaneously experiencing the most emotionally intense situation they may ever face. The combination frequently proves devastating, leading to the well-documented pattern of men falling apart after breakups in ways that shock their ex-partners, who have assumed their emotional stoicism meant they cared less. The man cared intensely but lacked any mechanism for processing the loss because he never developed emotional literacy skills or relationships that could support him through it.

The remedy requires building infrastructure that can support male emotional development outside the crucible of romantic relationships. This means creating contexts where men can practice emotional articulation with lower stakes and more patience than intimate partnerships allow. Men's groups focused specifically on developing emotional literacy have emerged as one promising model, providing structured formats for practicing feeling identification, vocabulary building, and narrative construction with other men who share the same developmental starting point. These groups work precisely because they remove the gender performance dynamics that make emotional learning feel threatening to masculine identity, when everyone in the room is struggling with the same skills, inadequacy becomes normalized rather than shameful. Therapeutic contexts provide another crucial site for building emotional literacy, offering expert guidance and a safe relationship for practicing new skills. However, men remain deeply resistant to therapy, viewing it as an admission of weakness rather than as skill-building, which means most never access this resource until crisis forces them into it. The cultural work of reframing emotional literacy as a learnable competence rather than an innate trait, and of creating male-friendly contexts for developing it, remains largely undone despite being essential for the well-being of both men and their intimate partners.

The contemporary moment presents both crisis and opportunity for male emotional development. The crisis lies in the growing gap between what intimate relationships require and what men are prepared to offer, creating relationship dissolution at unprecedented rates and widespread male isolation. The opportunity lies in the growing recognition that emotional literacy is a skill men can learn rather than a capacity they simply lack, and that building this skill serves men's own wellbeing as much as their partners'. Men with higher emotional literacy experience better physical health, lower rates of substance abuse, more satisfying relationships, greater career success, and longer lifespans. The benefits are not abstract or solely relational; they manifest in every domain of life. Yet capitalizing on this opportunity requires overcoming decades of socialization that taught men to view emotional incompetence as masculine and emotional learning as feminine, to experience emotions as threats to be suppressed rather than information to be processed, and to rely on romantic partners for emotional labor they should be capable of performing themselves. The work of building emotional literacy represents one of the most important developmental tasks facing contemporary men. Yet, most remain unaware they need it and are resistant to undertaking it even when the need becomes obvious through relationship failure and personal suffering.

Chapter 4: The Fear of Vulnerability: Breaking the Taboo

The paradox of masculine vulnerability reveals itself most acutely in what psychologists now call "approach-avoidance conflict", the simultaneous terror and desperate longing men experience when confronted with opportunities for genuine emotional exposure. A man may spend years in therapy learning to identify his feelings, developing emotional vocabulary, understanding his defensive patterns, and then find himself physiologically incapable of speaking when the moment arrives to reveal something deeply personal to his partner. His heart rate spikes beyond exercise levels, reaching the biological panic threshold. His hands tremble. His throat constricts as if his body itself is preventing the words from emerging. This is not resistance in the psychological sense, not defiance or stubbornness. This is the autonomic nervous system staging a mutiny, treating emotional disclosure as if it were mortal danger requiring immediate fight-or-flight activation. Research conducted by Dr. Matthew Lieberman at UCLA using neuroimaging technology demonstrates that when men anticipate emotional vulnerability, their amygdalae light up with activity patterns identical to those observed during physical threat assessment. The male brain, shaped by decades of conditioning, quite literally interprets emotional exposure as a survival threat, triggering ancient defensive systems designed to protect against predators, not protect against intimacy.

This neurobiological reality helps explain why men can intellectually understand that vulnerability strengthens relationships, can genuinely desire deeper connection, can recognize that their emotional guardedness creates distance, and yet find themselves absolutely unable to cross the threshold when opportunity presents itself. The man who promises himself he will finally talk to his wife about his childhood trauma finds himself making jokes instead when she asks how therapy went. The father who wants desperately to tell his adult son he is proud manufactures an excuse to leave the room when emotion threatens to surface. The friend who needs support sits silently while others share their struggles, then drives home, berating himself for cowardice. These are not failures of intention or commitment. These are men whose sympathetic nervous systems override their conscious intentions, flooding their bodies with adrenaline and cortisol that make authentic disclosure physiologically overwhelming. The shame that follows such moments compounds the original problem, creating a vicious cycle wherein the inability to be vulnerable generates shame that becomes yet another secret requiring concealment, further reinforcing the pattern. Understanding this mechanism is essential because it reframes what appears to be deliberate emotional withholding as a genuine disability requiring compassionate intervention rather than frustrated accusation.

The Social Geometry of Male Self-Disclosure

The contexts in which men can and cannot access vulnerability follow remarkably predictable patterns that illuminate the social architecture supporting or undermining emotional expression. Men universally report finding vulnerability easiest in what sociologists' term "side-by-side" contexts, situations where emotional disclosure occurs while engaged in parallel activity rather than face-to-face conversation. The classic example is the long drive, where men separated by decades of emotional distance somehow manage profound conversations while both staring forward at the highway. Construction sites, fishing trips, running together, working on cars, playing video games, these activity-centered contexts seem to bypass the vulnerability panic response that face-to-face emotional conversations trigger. The physical arrangement matters tremendously. Direct eye contact during emotional disclosure activates threat-detection systems in male brains far more intensely than it does in female brains, creating what researchers describe as "approach cues" that feel confrontational rather than connective. The man experiences the searching gaze of someone who loves him as interrogation rather than invitation, triggering defensive systems that slam shut precisely when opening would serve him best.

This pattern creates significant relationship challenges because women typically find face-to-face conversation the natural context for emotional intimacy, interpreting averted gaze or divided attention as disrespect or disengagement rather than recognizing these as enabling conditions for male disclosure. When a woman says she wants to "talk" and sits down facing her partner expectantly, she has inadvertently created the precise conditions under which his vulnerability capacity collapses. The man reads her body language, the direct gaze, the expectant posture, the focused attention, as demands for performance rather than connection invitations. His physiology responds accordingly, preparing for evaluation rather than intimacy. Contrast this with the same couple hiking together, both facing the trail ahead, conversation emerging organically from the rhythm of walking. In this configuration, the man's disclosure system can activate because the physical arrangement signals collaboration rather than examination. He can reveal fear about his father's declining health, uncertainty about his career trajectory, or loneliness within the relationship itself, admissions that would be impossible across the kitchen table but flow naturally on the trail. Women who understand this social geometry can create exponentially more opportunities for genuine male vulnerability by structuring connection opportunities around shared activity rather than dedicated conversation time.

The temporal dimension of vulnerability also follows distinct patterns for men. Immediate disclosure feels impossible, but delayed disclosure, sometimes weeks or months after an event, becomes accessible once the emotional intensity has diminished and cognitive processing has occurred. A man cannot talk about being passed over for promotion the day it happens. Still, three months later, he might casually mention feeling devastated by it during a conversation about something else entirely. This delayed processing frustrates partners who want real-time emotional access, but it reflects genuine differences in emotional processing speed and intensity tolerance. Men typically require what researchers call "emotional cooling periods" during which they process experiences internally, reducing them to manageable intensity before external disclosure becomes possible. Attempting to force premature disclosure simply triggers the panic response, shutting down communication entirely. Women who recognize this pattern can maintain connection through the cooling period without demanding immediate access, then remain alert for the delayed disclosure when it finally arrives, often obliquely and easily missed if not listening carefully.

Vulnerability Hierarchies and Selective Disclosure

Not all vulnerabilities carry equal psychological weight for men, and understanding the hierarchy of male disclosure fears reveals which emotional territories remain most dangerous and therefore most rigorously defended. At the apex of male vulnerability terror sits anything that could be interpreted as weakness in domains culturally coded as masculine competencies: financial struggle, sexual difficulty, physical inadequacy, professional failure, and the inability to protect or provide. A man will disclose childhood abuse, depression, loneliness, or grief before he will admit he cannot afford something his partner wants, that he experiences erectile dysfunction, that he feels physically intimidated by another man, that he is failing at work, or that he cannot fix a problem his family depends on him to solve. These admissions strike at the core of masculine identity in ways that other vulnerabilities, however painful, simply do not. Research conducted by Dr. Ronald Levant examining patterns of male self-disclosure found that men consistently ranked financial and sexual vulnerabilities as the most shame-inducing admissions, with willingness to disclose these concerns ranking significantly lower than willingness to disclose mental health struggles, emotional pain, or relationship dissatisfaction.

This hierarchy creates a peculiar situation in which a man might appear to be making progress with vulnerability, sharing feelings more openly, acknowledging fears, admitting uncertainty, while still maintaining absolute fortification around the vulnerabilities he experiences as most identity-threatening. A husband might discuss his anxiety and depression with remarkable openness while concealing from his wife that they are two months behind on the mortgage because he cannot bear to reveal his financial inadequacy. A father might speak movingly about his emotional distance from his own father while never mentioning that he feels like a failure as a provider because his income has stagnated. The selective disclosure creates a false sense of progress that obscures the remaining fortifications around the most shame-laden territories. Partners often misinterpret this as evidence that the man is "still hiding something" or being deliberately deceptive, when in fact he is operating at the absolute edge of his vulnerability capacity. Pushing harder in these domains does not produce a breakthrough; it makes a breakdown, as the man's defensive systems interpret the pressure as confirmation that his deepest fears about his inadequacy are shared by the person, he most hoped would contradict them.

Understanding this hierarchy allows women to recognize partial progress as genuine achievement while also understanding that certain territories may require years of careful approach rather than confrontation. The man who cannot admit financial struggle might be able to discuss "concerns about the future" or "pressure about work" as intermediate steps toward the core admission. The husband who cannot reveal sexual difficulty might be able to talk about "feeling disconnected physically" or "worrying about disappointing you" before naming the specific fear. These oblique approaches might feel frustratingly indirect to women who value clarity and directness. Still, they represent the only viable path for men whose defenses cannot withstand frontal assault on their most protected vulnerabilities. Paradoxically, the willingness to accept indirect disclosure and partial vulnerability often enables eventual direct admission, because the man experiences being met with compassion at the edge of his capacity, which slowly expands what that capacity can encompass.

The Witnessing Problem and Response Scripts

Perhaps the most confounding aspect of male vulnerability for women involves what happens after disclosure occurs. A man finally, painfully shares something deeply personal, fear, hurt, shame, longing, and the woman responds with exactly the emotional attunement and support she would want to receive, only to watch him become more distant and defended rather than more connected. This bewildering response pattern stems from what psychologists' term "vulnerability hangover", the intense shame and regret that many men experience after emotional disclosure, even when the disclosure is received with perfect compassion. The man's nervous system, having interpreted vulnerability as dangerous exposure, responds to the aftermath of disclosure as if he has revealed tactical weakness to an enemy. His defenses mobilize to prevent future exposure, leading to withdrawal, minimization of what was shared, or even anger at the partner for "making" him be vulnerable. The woman, expecting that vulnerability would create closeness, instead confronts inexplicable distance and feels punished for responding exactly as requested. This cycle devastates relationships because it creates a double bind: the man needs vulnerability to feel connected, but the act of being vulnerable triggers defensive systems that destroy connection.

The vulnerability hangover is intensified by the profound discomfort men experience with being witnessed in emotional distress without being offered solutions or action steps. When a man shares pain and receives empathetic listening, his instrumental orientation interprets this as being trapped in useless suffering rather than recognizing emotional witness as valuable in itself. Research by Dr. Annette Stanton examining gender differences in coping mechanisms found that men experience significantly higher distress when prevented from taking action on problems compared to women, who report comfort from emotional processing even when circumstances remain unchanged. For men, being seen in pain without moving toward resolution creates a compounding vulnerability, not only is the original problem still present, but now someone has witnessed their inability to solve it. This witnesses-to-helplessness dynamic violates a core masculine script about never revealing incapacity, triggering secondary shame that overwhelms whatever relief the initial disclosure might have provided. The man's partner, following the feminine script of providing empathetic presence as the primary gift during suffering, inadvertently intensifies his distress by refusing to shift into problem-solving mode.

This mismatch in response scripts creates a situation where women must learn to violate their own instincts about proper caregiving to effectively support male vulnerability. When a man shares pain, the most helpful response often involves acknowledging the feeling briefly, then asking what would help or offering concrete assistance rather than extended emotional processing. This can feel dismissive to women, who experience sustained emotional attention as the highest form of care, but it matches male needs far more accurately. A response like "That sounds incredibly difficult. What would make this easier? Is there anything I can do to help?" often lands better than extended empathetic reflection, because it acknowledges the emotion while moving toward the action phase that male nervous systems require to metabolize vulnerability. This is not because men are less emotional or more superficial, but because their regulatory systems are organized around different principles. Understanding this allows women to provide support that reduces rather than intensifies vulnerability hangover, making future disclosure less terrifying and more likely.

Comparative Vulnerability and the Zero-Sum Error

One of the most toxic patterns surrounding male vulnerability involves what researchers call "comparative suffering", the implicit or explicit suggestion that because someone else experiences greater hardship, the man's own struggles are illegitimate or unworthy of attention. Men are exquisitely sensitive to this dynamic, having internalized the cultural message that masculine suffering ranks low in any hierarchy of worthy concern. When a man tentatively reveals difficulty, stress at work, exhaustion, feeling overwhelmed, and receives a response that references others' greater challenges, his vulnerability system interprets this as confirmation that his pain does not merit acknowledgment. The response might be subtle: "Well, at least you do not have to deal with..." or "That must be hard, but think about people who..." or even sharing a news story about someone facing catastrophe. Each of these moves communicates that the man's vulnerability has been weighed and found insufficient, triggering instant defensive closure. The man who was attempting connection retreats into isolation, having learned that disclosure produces dismissal rather than recognition.

This comparative framework reflects what psychologists term the "zero-sum error" about suffering, the mistaken belief that acknowledging one person's pain somehow diminishes or invalidates another's. In reality, suffering is not a competitive domain where validation must be rationed according to objective severity rankings. A man's experience of overwhelming caring for aging parents while managing demanding work is genuine suffering, regardless of whether someone else faces starvation or war. The pain of chronic loneliness is real, irrespective of whether someone else experiences homelessness. Yet men universally report having their suffering comparatively minimized throughout their lives, creating a powerful expectation that vulnerability will be met with perspective-giving dismissal rather than simple recognition. This history makes male disclosure an act of extraordinary courage, because the man is risking not just exposure but explicit confirmation that his internal experience does not matter sufficiently to warrant attention or care.

Women can interrupt this pattern by practicing what psychologists call "non-comparative recognition", the ability to acknowledge suffering without immediately contextualizing it within a hierarchy of worse situations. When a man shares difficulty, the response "That sounds really hard" without qualification or comparison communicates that his experience has inherent validity independent of where it ranks against other hardships. This simple shift can be remarkably difficult for women who have been trained to minimize their own suffering through constant comparison and who therefore reflexively apply the same diminishing framework to others. Breaking this pattern requires conscious practice, especially when the man's disclosed struggle seems objectively minor or when the woman herself is managing challenges that appear more severe. The discipline of receiving another's pain without evaluating its comparative worthiness represents a profound act of respect that many men have never experienced, creating possibilities for vulnerability they have never before accessed.

Vulnerability Timing and the Crisis Paradox

A particularly confounding pattern in male vulnerability involves what researchers term the "crisis paradox", the observation that men often become most defended and least accessible precisely when circumstances would logically suggest maximum need for support. The man who loses his job becomes withdrawn and irritable rather than seeking comfort. The father whose child is diagnosed with a serious illness grows cold and distant rather than reaching for connection. The husband, facing his own mortality after a health scare, intensifies his emotional fortification rather than opening to the reality of his fear. This counterintuitive response bewilders partners who naturally increase their offers of support during a crisis, only to encounter unprecedented defensiveness that makes the crisis even more isolating for both parties. The pattern stems from the fact that genuine crisis triggers maximum vulnerability at precisely the moment when the man's entire psychological structure is organized around projecting competence and containing distress. The worse the situation, the more desperately the man feels he must appear capable of handling it, because to reveal struggle during crisis would confirm his deepest fear, that he fundamentally lacks what is required, that he is inadequate to meet the demands of his role.

Crisis vulnerability operates according to distinctly different principles than everyday emotional disclosure. During normal circumstances, a man might slowly develop the capacity for sharing struggles because the stakes feel manageable and he can calibrate disclosure to his tolerance level. Crisis eliminates this controlled approach, demanding vulnerability at a scale that overwhelms his regulatory capacity. The man experiencing job loss knows his identity as a provider is under direct assault, making admission of struggle feel like accepting total failure rather than processing a difficult experience. His defenses mobilize not despite the severity of the situation but precisely because of it. He cannot afford vulnerability when his entire sense of masculine adequacy hangs in the balance. This creates a tragic dynamic where the man most needs support at exactly the moment he is least able to receive it, and where the partner most wants to provide care at exactly the moment it will be most strenuously rejected. Breaking through this pattern requires understanding that crisis demands different approaches than everyday vulnerability work.

During an acute crisis, direct demands for emotional disclosure typically fail because the man's defensive systems are operating at maximum capacity. More effective approaches involve what psychologists call "instrumental intimacy", providing concrete support that communicates care without requiring vulnerability. Taking over specific tasks, managing logistics, solving practical problems, or simply maintaining a calm presence without demanding emotional access gives the man space to stabilize before disclosure becomes possible. Research by Dr. Shelley Taylor on stress responses found that men in crisis show decreased stress markers when allowed to engage in goal-directed activity rather than emotional processing, suggesting that practical engagement supports recovery more effectively than attempted emotional connection during acute phases. This is not about abandoning someone in crisis but about meeting them where their regulatory capacity exists rather than where we wish it existed. The time for emotional processing comes later, often weeks or months after the crisis passes, when the man's defenses have de-escalated sufficiently to permit the delayed vulnerability that the acute crisis made impossible.

Chapter 5: Communication Breakdown: Ego, Fear, and Misunderstanding

The single most destructive force in modern heterosexual relationships is not infidelity, financial stress, or sexual incompatibility. It is the cascading failure of communication that occurs when a woman asks a simple question and receives an answer so comprehensively disconnected from what she asked that both parties leave the interaction feeling misunderstood, dismissed, and increasingly convinced the other person operates with fundamentally different intentions. These failures follow predictable patterns, yet they remain baffling to both participants because each person genuinely believes they are communicating clearly while the other is being deliberately obtuse or hurtful. The breakdown occurs not at the level of vocabulary or even emotional literacy, but at the deeper level of what communication is supposed to accomplish. For most women, communication serves primarily relational functions, it creates connection, processes experience, establishes shared understanding, and regulates emotional proximity. For most men, communication serves mainly instrumental functions, it conveys information, solves problems, establishes hierarchy, and manages external threats. When these fundamentally different communication purposes collide without either party recognizing the collision, the result is not mere misunderstanding but something more corrosive: the gradual conviction that one's partner is actively choosing not to meet basic relational needs.

The Meaning-Making Divide

Consider a common scenario that plays out in thousands of households nightly. A woman arrives home visibly upset and begins recounting a workplace conflict in detailed narrative form, describing not just the events but the interpersonal dynamics, the history of relationships involved, her moment-by-moment emotional responses, and her uncertainty about how to interpret ambiguous social signals. She speaks for perhaps eight or ten minutes, her partner listening with what appears to be attention. When she finishes, he offers a single declarative sentence: "You should talk to HR." She stares at him, feeling as though he has not heard a word she said. He stares back, genuinely confused about why she looks hurt, convinced he has just provided a valuable solution to the problem she spent ten minutes explaining. Both are correct within their own framework, and both are catastrophically missing what the other person needed from the exchange. She needed collaborative sense-making, the joint construction of meaning through conversational exploration that would help her understand her own reactions, validate her perceptions, and process the emotional impact of the conflict. He heard a problem requiring a solution and offered the most efficient path to resolution. Neither recognizes that they were having two entirely different conversations disguised as the same interaction.

This meaning-making divide extends far beyond the complaint about men offering solutions instead of empathy, which has become such a relationship cliché that most men now know they are supposed to avoid it, even if they do not understand why their solutions are unwelcome. The deeper issue involves fundamentally different epistemologies, different theories about how understanding itself is constructed. In the feminine conversational tradition, understanding emerges through a dialectical process: a speaker presents an experience, the listener reflects their interpretation, the speaker refines or corrects, the listener offers parallel experiences or alternative framings, and through this back-and-forth movement, both parties arrive at a richer, more nuanced understanding than either possessed initially. The conversation itself is the method of knowing. Truth is not transmitted from speaker to listener but co-created between them. This process requires time, tolerance for ambiguity, comfort with contradiction, and the willingness to hold multiple interpretations simultaneously without rushing toward resolution. The value lies not in concluding but in the quality of exploration itself. For many men, this process feels interminable and pointless. Their epistemology is fundamentally different: understanding means identifying the essential facts, eliminating irrelevant details, determining causation, and reaching a conclusion that enables effective action. The conversation is merely a vehicle for information transfer, not an end in itself. Efficiency is valued over thoroughness, clarity over nuance, decisive judgment over sustained ambiguity.

When these conflicting epistemologies collide, both parties experience the other's approach as not just different but actively wrong. The woman experiences the man's rush to conclusion as dismissive of complexity, as intellectually lazy, as unwilling to truly grapple with the messy reality of human experience. She interprets his desire for resolution as avoidance of the difficult emotional work required for genuine understanding. The man experiences the woman's extended exploration as circular and unproductive, as wallowing rather than progressing, as refusing to make the tough decisions necessary to move forward. He interprets her resistance to his conclusions as a sign that she does not actually want help but rather wants to remain stuck in complaint. Neither recognizes that they are measuring success by completely different metrics. She evaluates the conversation's success by how connected and understood she feels afterward, by whether her emotional experience was witnessed and validated, and by whether the joint exploration expanded her perspective. He evaluates success by whether useful information was exchanged, whether a viable course of action was identified, and whether the problem is closer to being resolved. By her metrics, his approach is a comprehensive failure. By his metrics, her approach never even begins addressing the actual issue.

Ego Defense Through Information Control

The masculine ego structure creates a particularly insidious communication pattern in which men unconsciously manage what information gets shared based on how that information reflects on their competence, status, and adequacy. This is not the same as conscious lying or deliberate deception, though it can shade into those territories. Rather, it represents an automatic filtering system in which information that threatens masculine self-concept gets minimized, reframed, or withheld without the man necessarily being aware he is doing so. Research in social psychology on ego-protective processing demonstrates that all humans engage in selective attention and memory based on self-concept threats. Still, masculine socialization creates particular vulnerabilities around admissions of incompetence, dependence, confusion, or failure. When a man is asked about something that touched on these zones, "How did the presentation go?" "What did the doctor say?" "Did you figure out the problem with the car?", his response system automatically calculates not just what happened but how the truthful answer positions him in terms of masculine adequacy. If the true answer threatens that positioning, his brain rapidly generates alternative framings that preserve status while remaining technically factual.

This produces communication that women experience as evasive or dishonest, but men experience as straightforward, because the man genuinely believes he is answering accurately. The presentation that received critical feedback gets described as "fine" or "it went okay" because acknowledging public professional failure feels intolerable. The man's attention automatically focuses on the two positive comments while the eight concerns fade from memory. The doctor's visit, where he received a troubling diagnosis, gets reduced to logistical details about follow-up appointments, not because he is consciously hiding the diagnosis but because his psychological immune system has already begun minimizing its emotional significance before he even gets home. The car problem he could not solve gets reframed as "still working on it" rather than "I have no idea what is wrong," because admitting mechanical incompetence violates a core masculine competency domain. In each case, the man would likely pass a polygraph test if asked whether he answered honestly, because within his own internal experience, he did. The automatic reframing happens so quickly and smoothly that it feels like simply reporting reality. Women, however, experience a growing sense that they are receiving edited versions of their partner's life, that significant information is being withheld or distorted, and that they cannot trust what they are told. This destroys intimacy far more thoroughly than occasional deliberate lies, because it is constant, pervasive, and invisible to the person doing it.

The information control pattern becomes particularly toxic during conflicts, when ego protection systems activate most intensely. During an argument about emotional neglect, a woman presents specific instances when she needed support, and her partner was absent or dismissive. In her framework, she is providing data points that illustrate a pattern requiring acknowledgment and repair. In his framework, he is being presented with evidence of his failure as a partner, which activates intense shame and defensive reactions. His ego-protection system immediately begins generating alternative explanations that preserve his self-concept as a good partner: those instances were not as significant as she is claiming, his responses were reasonable given what he knew at the time, she is being overly sensitive or misremembering the context, she is cherry-picking negative examples while ignoring all the times he was supportive. These defensive reframings are not calculated strategies to win the argument. They feel true to him because his psychological immune system needs them to be true. The alternative, accepting that he genuinely failed his partner in moments when she needed him most, threatens his entire self-concept. So his brain automatically constructs a narrative in which he is being unfairly attacked rather than appropriately held accountable. The woman watches this defensive reconstruction happening in real time and experiences it as gaslighting, as a deliberate attempt to make her doubt her own perceptions. Both parties leave the interaction more entrenched in their positions, more convinced that the other is operating in bad faith.

The Subtext Blindness Problem

One of the most maddening aspects of male-female communication breakdown involves what linguists call "pragmatic competence", the ability to understand implied meaning, emotional subtext, and indirect speech acts. Women generally develop sophisticated pragmatic competence through years of conversational practice in which direct statements are often face-threatening or socially inappropriate, requiring the use of indirect forms that preserve plausible deniability while still conveying actual intent. A woman learns to express anger through studied politeness, to communicate hurt through carefully casual remarks about unrelated topics, to test relationship security through seemingly innocuous questions loaded with significance. This indirect communication style serves important social functions in female peer groups and family systems, allowing difficult truths to be conveyed while maintaining surface harmony and giving recipients room to save face. However, this same communication style becomes catastrophically ineffective with partners who have not developed equivalent pragmatic skills and who interpret language far more literally than intended.

When a woman says "Do whatever you want" in a tone dripping with resentment, she is not actually giving permission. She is expressing anger about not being considered in a decision while avoiding confrontation. The pragmatics are clear to anyone fluent in indirect speech: this is a complaint disguised as permission, meant to be recognized as such and responded to with apology and course correction. Many men, however, hear literal permission and proceed with the original plan, genuinely confused when their partner becomes furious. They missed the subtext entirely, not because they are stupid or deliberately obtuse, but because they are operating with a different pragmatic framework in which words mean what they literally denote rather than serving as vehicles for emotional messages requiring interpretation. When a woman asks, "Are you really going to wear that?" she is not requesting information about his intentions. She is expressing disapproval and hoping he will change his outfit. When she says, "I guess I'll just handle it myself," she is not planning but issuing a complaint about unequal labor distribution. When she mentions that "Sarah's husband surprised her with flowers for no reason," she is not reporting celebrity gossip but expressing desire for spontaneous romantic gestures. Each of these utterances contains a clear meaning to someone fluent in pragmatic interpretation. Still, to someone operating with a more literal interpretive framework, they mean exactly what the words denote and nothing more.

This subtext blindness creates a devastating dynamic in which women feel unheard and invisible because their actual communications are being systematically misunderstood. In contrast, men feel perpetually confused and accused of failures they never saw coming because they are being held accountable for responding to messages they did not know were being sent. The woman becomes increasingly frustrated that she must spell out every need explicitly, which defeats the entire purpose of pragmatic communication, the point is that spontaneous understanding and intuitive responsiveness demonstrate true attentiveness and care. Being forced to state directly,

"I want you to plan a date night without me asking," makes the eventual date night feel hollow, because the value lies in the unprompted recognition of her need. The man, meanwhile, becomes increasingly defensive about being expected to be a mind-reader, about being criticized for taking people at their word, about the unfairness of a system in which he gets punished for supposed failures that were never clearly communicated in the first place. Both positions are valid within their own frameworks. The woman's need for intuitive attunement and spontaneous responsiveness is not excessive or unreasonable; it reflects how she was taught to demonstrate love and how she naturally interprets others' care. The man's frustration with unclear expectations and indirect communication is equally legitimate, he is being held to a standard he was never taught to meet, using skills he was never allowed to develop.

The Meta-Communication Failure

Perhaps the most pernicious communication breakdown occurs not in the content-level conversation but in the conversation about the conversation, what communication scholars call "meta-communication." When a relationship struggle involves communication itself, couples need to be able to discuss how they are talking to each other, what assumptions and needs they are bringing to their interactions, and what adjustments might help. However, attempting meta-communication requires both parties to step outside their immediate defensive reactions and examine their own communication patterns with some objectivity, which is precisely what people cannot do when ego and fear are fully activated. The conversation about why they cannot talk productively devolves into yet another example of talking unproductively, creating recursive loops where the solution attempt becomes a new instantiation of the original problem. A woman tries to explain that her partner's problem-solving responses make her feel unheard. He hears this as criticism of his attempts to help, activates his defensive systems, and responds by explaining why offering solutions is a reasonable response to someone presenting a problem. She experiences this defensive explanation as yet another example of him invalidating her feelings by prioritizing his perspective over her experience. He experiences her rejection of his explanation as proof that she does not want actual dialogue but only wants him to agree that he is wrong.

The meta-communication failure intensifies because each party believes they are being clear about what the real issue is. In contrast, the other party is equally convinced they understand the real problem, and it is not what their partner keeps claiming. The woman insists the problem is emotional attunement and feeling prioritized in his attention. The man insists the issue is unclear expectations and constantly moving goalposts. Both are partially correct, but neither can hold their partner's perspective simultaneously with their own long enough to find common ground. Instead, they engage in what psychologist John Gottman identified as "perpetual argument syndrome", having the same fight repeatedly because they are arguing about different things while using the same words. She says, "You never listen to me," meaning he does not provide the emotional presence and reflective engagement she needs. He hears "You never listen to me" as a factually false accusation, he clearly hears the words she says and retains the information. She says, "I need you to be more present," meaning she needs him to prioritize their relationship in his attention and energy allocation. He hears this as a demand for more time together and responds by noting all the time they already spend in the same physical space. The semantic mismatch goes unrecognized because both parties assume their meanings are obvious and the other person's alternative interpretation is a willful misunderstanding.

Breaking out of meta-communication failures requires skills that most couples lack: the ability to recognize when you are defending rather than understanding, the willingness to accurately represent your partner's perspective even when you disagree with it, the capacity to acknowledge that your partner's experience of your behavior might be valid even if it does not match your intentions, and the humility to consider that your communication style might genuinely not be working regardless of how natural it feels to you. These skills are difficult for anyone, but masculine defensive structures make them particularly challenging for men. Acknowledging that his communication approach is causing harm to his partner without being able to claim he intended that harm creates a cognitive bind: either he is incompetent at communication (threatening to ego) or he needs to fundamentally change how he operates (threatening to identity). Most men unconsciously choose a third option: insist that their communication is fine and their partner is being unreasonable. This resolves the cognitive dissonance while making the relationship problem unsolvable.

The Performance of Communication

The contemporary relationship landscape has produced a particularly insidious dynamic in which men learn to perform communication competence, to execute the behaviors associated with good partnership while remaining emotionally disengaged from the content. Sociologist Arlie Hochschild's research on "emotional labor" documented how service workers learn to display emotions they do not feel as part of job performance. A similar dynamic now operates in many long-term relationships, where men learn through repeated conflict that certain responses avoid arguments even if those responses feel hollow or dishonest. The man who sits through his partner's work story and asks follow-up questions he does not care about, who remembers to say "that must be difficult" at appropriate intervals, who has learned that ninety seconds of simulated listening prevents an hour-long conflict about never listening. This man has discovered that communication can be successfully performed without genuine engagement. He learns the script: make eye contact, put away phone, ask the right prompts, mirror her emotional words back to her. If executed correctly, these behaviors satisfy the observable criteria for good communication while requiring no actual emotional availability or relational investment.

Women generally sense this performative quality even when they cannot articulate what feels off. The right words are being said, the appropriate behaviors are being displayed, but something essential is missing, the sense of genuine mutual presence, of authentic interest, of real emotional exchange. The disconnect between perfect surface communication and hollow underlying connection creates a particularly crazy-making situation, because the woman cannot point to any specific failure. Her partner is doing all the things relationship advice claims constitute good communication. He is listening, asking questions, reflecting feelings, and offering support. Yet she feels more alone than when he openly ignored her, because at least that was honest. The performance of intimacy without its substance is more alienating than the absence of performance altogether. The man, meanwhile, feels increasingly resentful that his efforts are never enough, that even when he does everything she claims to want, she remains unsatisfied. From his perspective, he is making genuine sacrifices, enduring conversations he finds tedious, suppressing his desire to offer solutions, and engaging in emotional processing that feels unnatural and exhausting. That these efforts feel like sacrifices rather than authentic expressions of care reveals the fundamental problem, but that awareness remains inaccessible to him because examining it would require acknowledging the emotional disconnection he is working so hard to conceal.

The performance of communication becomes most visible during couples therapy, where men often prove remarkably adept at learning the language of emotional intelligence and relational awareness while remaining fundamentally unchanged. They absorb the vocabulary of attachment theory, recognize their defensive patterns in abstract discussions, and demonstrate impressive insight into their own psychological processes during sessions. Then they return home and replicate the same behaviors that brought them to therapy, because intellectual understanding of communication principles does not automatically translate to embodied change in communication practice. The man can explain why his partner's bid for connection deserves attention and describe his tendency to offer solutions instead of empathy, then, in the next argument, offer solutions instead of empathy without any awareness of the discrepancy. He has learned to talk about communication in therapy without learning to communicate differently in his relationship. This pattern frustrates therapists and partners alike, creating the sense that the man is not trying or is sabotaging treatment, when often he is genuinely confused about why his obvious progress in therapy is not translating to improvement at home. The gap between knowledge and practice, between understanding communication concepts and spontaneously communicating effectively, remains invisible to him because he has been conditioned to measure success by intellectual mastery rather than behavioral change.

The Language of Repair and the Apology Impasse

Perhaps nowhere does communication breakdown more completely than in the aftermath of conflict, when repair attempts that could restore connection instead become new sites of injury and misunderstanding. The structure of an effective apology requires several components: acknowledgment of the specific harm caused, acceptance of responsibility without defensive justification, expression of genuine remorse, and commitment to behavioral change. Women generally learn these components through extensive relationship repair practice starting in childhood, where maintaining friendships demands sophisticated capacities for apology and forgiveness. Men often receive no such training, learning instead that apology represents a status loss, an admission of defeat in hierarchical competition, a position of vulnerability that invites further attack. When a man does offer an apology, it frequently takes forms that violate every principle of effective repair while feeling perfectly adequate to him: "I'm sorry you got upset" (acknowledging her reaction rather than his behavior), "I'm sorry but you also..." (canceling responsibility through immediate counteraccusation), "I'm sorry, okay?" (performing apology as demanded compliance rather than genuine remorse). Each of these formulations destroys repair opportunities while allowing the man to feel he has met the requirement for apology. When his partner responds with continued anger, he experiences this as punitive and unreasonable, he apologized, she needs to move on.

The deeper issue underlying the apology impasse involves fundamentally different understandings of what apology accomplishes. For most women, apology is not simply a social ritual marking the end of conflict but a relational act that requires emotional vulnerability, genuine self-reflection, and authentic remorse. The apology itself is valuable primarily because it demonstrates that the apologizer understands the impact of their behavior, takes responsibility for that impact regardless of intention, feels genuine regret about causing harm, and has reflected sufficiently to commit to different behavior in the future. These components cannot be rushed or performed; they require actual emotional work and real self-examination. For many men, apology functions more pragmatically: it is the required statement that resolves conflict and allows forward movement. The emphasis falls on efficiency rather than depth, on getting past the conflict rather than fully processing it. When his partner rejects his initial apology attempt as inadequate, the man often becomes frustrated and defensive, interpreting her insistence on a "better" apology as pointless emotional theater or deliberate punishment. He genuinely does not understand what more she wants beyond the words "I'm sorry," because his framework does not include the concept that apology quality matters, that the emotional truth beneath the words matters, that an inadequate apology can be worse than no apology.

This creates particularly painful dynamics after betrayals or serious violations, when the woman desperately needs her partner to demonstrate real understanding of what he has done and genuine remorse for having done it. At the same time, the man experiences her continued hurt despite his apologies as evidence that forgiveness is impossible and he will be permanently punished regardless of what he says. Both experiences are valid. She genuinely needs something beyond words to believe the relationship can be repaired, she needs to see evidence of emotional reckoning, of real remorse, of the kind of authentic vulnerability that suggests he has confronted what his behavior meant. He genuinely feels trapped in an impossible situation where no apology will ever be sufficient, where he is expected to perform emotional displays that feel false to him. Where the cost of admission is permanent relegation to the inferior position in a hierarchy he did not know existed. Neither can access the other's framework, so they remain locked in recursive cycles where his inadequate apologies increase her despair, and her rejection of his apologies increases his defensive resentment, making genuine repair less likely with each iteration.

The communication breakdown surrounding ego, fear, and misunderstanding is not a problem that can be solved through better communication techniques, because the breakdown occurs at a level before technique, in the fundamentally different purposes, assumptions, and skills that men and women bring to communicative interactions. No amount of "I statements" or active listening training addresses the reality that for one party, communication primarily builds connection, while for the other, it mainly exchanges information. No conflict resolution framework repairs the fact that one person has been trained their entire life in pragmatic interpretation and indirect speech, while the other person operates with a literal interpretive framework. No relationship advice resolves the fundamental tension between needing to feel spontaneously understood while partnered with someone who requires explicit instruction. These are not failures of will or effort but consequences of profoundly different developmental trajectories that create genuinely incompatible communication systems operating under the illusion of shared language. Understanding this does not make the problem disappear. Still, it shifts the framework from blame to tragedy, from assuming someone is being deliberately difficult to recognizing that both parties are doing their best within systems that were never designed to interface successfully.

Chapter 6: The Paradox of Connection: Craving Yet Resisting

The most confounding aspect of masculine psychology reveals itself not in what men avoid, but in what they simultaneously pursue and sabotage. A man spends months building toward a moment of genuine intimacy with his partner, opening incrementally, lowering defenses, allowing himself to be truly seen, and then, precisely when that intimacy reaches its apex, he engineers its destruction. He picks a fight over something trivial, suddenly announces he needs space, becomes emotionally unavailable for days, or manufactures a crisis that re-establishes distance. The woman watches this pattern repeat, unable to comprehend why the very connection he seemed to desperately want becomes intolerable the moment it is achieved. This is not a simple commitment phobia or fear of vulnerability repackaged. This is a far more complex psychological bind in which men experience connection itself as simultaneously necessary for psychological survival and threatening to their sense of autonomous selfhood. The result is a perpetual oscillation between pursuing intimacy and fleeing from it, creating relational whiplash that leaves both partners exhausted and confused.

The Developmental Origins of Ambivalent Attachment

The roots of this paradox extend into early childhood development, specifically into the process psychologists' term "separation-individuation", the critical developmental task in which a child establishes psychological autonomy while maintaining emotional connection to caregivers. Research conducted by developmental psychologist Janet Surrey at the Stone Center has documented that boys and girls navigate this process through fundamentally different pathways, with lasting consequences for adult intimacy patterns. Girls typically achieve individuation through maintaining and renegotiating connection, learning that they can be both separate selves and deeply connected to others simultaneously. Their developmental trajectory involves differentiation within a relationship rather than differentiation through separation. Boys, conversely, are pushed toward a more radical severing of early attachment bonds, particularly with their primary caregiver, who is most often female. To establish masculine identity, boys learn they must reject identification with the feminine, which in practical terms means learning to experience closeness with women as threatening to their emerging sense of manhood.

Studies utilizing longitudinal observation of mother-son dyads reveal that this enforced separation begins astonishingly early, often by age two or three, when boys are discouraged from seeking comfort, told to be brave instead of cry, and pushed toward independence at ages when girls are still encouraged to maintain close physical and emotional proximity with caregivers. The psychological consequence is that boys develop what attachment researchers call "avoidant attachment patterns" not necessarily because of neglect or abuse, but as an adaptive response to cultural demands that they establish masculine identity through emotional self-sufficiency. The boy learns that needing connection is dangerous, that depending on another person makes him vulnerable to rejection or humiliation, and that the safest psychological position is one of defended independence. Yet this learning occurs on top of the biological and psychological reality that all humans require connection for emotional regulation and psychological health. The result is not that boys stop needing attachment, but that they develop profound ambivalence about that need, experiencing it as both essential and shameful, both desperately wanted and fundamentally threatening.

This developmental foundation creates men who approach adult intimacy with what psychologists' term "anxious-avoidant" patterns, simultaneously craving the very closeness they are compelled to resist. The man genuinely longs for the emotional safety and acceptance that deep partnership offers, recognizes intellectually that vulnerability and interdependence are necessary for the kind of love he wants, and yet experiences every movement toward genuine intimacy as an existential threat to his autonomy. His psychological immune system interprets connection as infection rather than nourishment, triggering defensive responses precisely when he is most exposed. The tragedy is that these defenses activate outside conscious awareness. The man does not experience himself as deliberately sabotaging intimacy. He experiences a sudden, urgent need for space as a legitimate self-preservation response. He perceives the trivial conflict he initiates as genuinely important rather than recognizing it as a pretext for re-establishing distance. His psychological defense mechanisms have become so automatic that they feel like authentic responses to real threats rather than outdated protective patterns responding to long-ago dangers.

The Engulfment Terror and Masculinity Maintenance

The specific fear that drives men away from achieved intimacy centers on what psychoanalytic theory terms "engulfment anxiety", the terror of being psychologically absorbed or obliterated by merger with another person. This is not a metaphorical concern but visceral panic that manifests in physical symptoms: chest tightness, difficulty breathing, urgent need to escape. For men, this engulfment terror carries particular associations with loss of masculine identity, because the cultural definition of manhood remains so thoroughly tied to independence, self-containment, and autonomous agency. To need another person deeply, to allow that person to see one's full interior landscape, to depend on them for emotional regulation or validation, these experiences activate ancient prohibitions against masculine dependence that feel like threats to manhood itself. Research conducted by masculinity scholar Michael Kimmel documents how men describe moments of deep intimacy using language typically reserved for experiences of unmanning: "losing myself," "being swallowed up," "disappearing into her needs." The metaphors reveal the underlying terror, that intimacy with a woman threatens to reverse the fundamental developmental achievement of masculine separation, pulling him back into a feminine orbit that feels incompatible with male identity.

This terror intensifies in proportion to the actual quality of the connection achieved. Paradoxically, the more genuine and profound the intimacy, the more threatening it becomes, because deep connection makes visible just how much the man actually depends on his partner for emotional sustenance, identity validation, and psychological coherence. Shallow connection allows him to maintain the fiction of independence, he could walk away, he does not really need her, he remains fundamentally self-sufficient. Profound connection destroys this protective fiction. It makes viscerally obvious that he has become dependent, that she now carries pieces of him that he cannot retrieve, that his emotional equilibrium requires her ongoing presence. For men trained to experience dependence as weakness, this realization triggers existential panic. The immediate response is to re-establish the fiction of independence through withdrawal, to prove to himself that he does not actually need what he has just admitted needing. He creates distance not because the intimacy felt bad, but precisely because it felt too good, good enough to reveal the depth of his dependence, which activates overwhelming shame about having violated masculine self-sufficiency mandates.

Women typically experience this withdrawal as rejection or punishment, assuming they did something wrong or that the intimacy was not as mutual as they believed. The man's retreat feels like evidence that he was faking a connection or that he discovered something about her that made him pull away. The withdrawal has nothing to do with her specific qualities or actions and everything to do with his inability to tolerate his own need. This creates a tragic misunderstanding in which the woman internalizes blame for the man's defensive reaction, often trying to fix imagined deficiencies in herself or the relationship rather than recognizing the issue as his regulatory failure. The man, meanwhile, usually cannot articulate or even consciously remember the engulfment terror driving his behavior. He experiences vague discomfort, sudden irritation with aspects of the relationship that previously felt fine, and restlessness that gets interpreted as evidence he needs more individual space or freedom. His defensive system has successfully obscured the true threat, his own need, by reframing the problem as something external that requires adjustment rather than an internal psychological bind requiring examination.

The Cyclical Pattern of Pursuit and Withdrawal

This ambivalent attachment creates a characteristic relational pattern that therapist's term "the pursuer-distancer cycle," though understanding it through the lens of masculine connection paradox reveals dynamics invisible in generic relationship models. The cycle begins with a period of pursuit, often initiated by the man after a period of distance has successfully re-established his sense of independence. Having achieved psychological separation, his attachment needs re-emerge without triggering engulfment panic. He becomes affectionate, communicative, sexually interested, and emotionally available. The woman, who has been experiencing painful abandonment during the distance phase, responds with relief and gratitude, opening herself to renewed connection. The couple enters a period of genuine intimacy characterized by vulnerability, shared experience, emotional attunement, and mutual dependence. This phase might last days, weeks, or even months, depending on the individual's capacity to tolerate need before it triggers defensive responses.

As intimacy deepens, the man begins experiencing subtle signals of engulfment anxiety, vague restlessness, irritation with behaviors he previously found endearing, feeling smothered by requests for time or attention that previously felt comfortable, perceiving normal relationship expectations as excessive demands. These signals exist beneath conscious awareness, manifesting as mood changes and cognitive distortions rather than explicit recognition of fear. The man does not think, "I am afraid of how much I need her." He believes "She is too needy," or "I need more time with friends," or "This relationship feels suffocating." His perception shifts to emphasize her demands and minimize his agency, reframing interdependence as one-directional dependence where she needs him but he does not need her. This cognitive distortion allows him to initiate withdrawal without confronting his own attachment vulnerability. He becomes less available, more critical, emotionally distant, and sexually disinterested. The woman, detecting this shift, typically responds by increasing pursuit, seeking reassurance, initiating conversations about the relationship, requesting more quality time, which the man experiences as confirmation that she is indeed too needy, validating his defensive reframing.

The cycle reaches its nadir when maximum distance has been established. The woman, exhausted by the pursuit that generates no response, withdraws into protective self-sufficiency or angry resentment. The man, having successfully reasserted independence, begins to feel safe enough for his attachment needs to re-emerge. But now he encounters a partner who has moved into protective distance, which activates his own abandonment fears. Suddenly, he pursues, initiating connection, expressing appreciation, demonstrating attentiveness, confused about why she is now unavailable when he is finally ready to connect. She experiences his renewed pursuit as manipulative or simply too late, unable to trust that his availability will persist beyond the immediate crisis of her withdrawal. Yet if she maintains distance long enough, his pursuit typically intensifies until she softens, and the cycle begins again. This pattern can persist for years or even decades, with neither partner recognizing it as a systematic defensive response to masculine ambivalence about need rather than evidence of incompatibility or relationship failure.

The Counterdependence Masquerade

A particularly sophisticated version of this paradox manifests in what psychologists term "counterdependent behavior", the strategic performance of extreme independence that functions to mask and manage profound underlying dependence. Counterdependent men do not simply withdraw from intimacy; they actively construct elaborate systems of self-sufficiency that create the appearance of needing nothing from anyone. They maintain extensive social networks but no truly intimate friendships. They pursue intensive hobbies, professional achievements, or physical challenges that consume time and attention. They cultivate an identity of rugged individualism, priding themselves on solving problems alone, never asking for help, and maintaining emotional equilibrium without support. This performance appears to outside observers, including partners, as genuine independence or even extreme autonomy. In reality, it represents hypervigilance against dependence, not the absence of need but its strenuous denial.

Research conducted by psychologist Robert Firestone on "fantasy bonds" in adult relationships reveals that counterdependent men often maintain what appears to be a committed partnership while ensuring that no genuine interdependence develops. They are physically present but emotionally absent, willing to perform relationship maintenance behaviors but resistant to actual vulnerability or mutual reliance. The relationship provides certain benefits, domestic comfort, sexual access, social legitimacy, companionship, without requiring the psychological risk of genuine dependence. The man believes he is protecting both himself and his partner through this emotional distance, if if she never becomes truly necessary to his psychological functioning, he can never be devastated by losing her. The defensive logic is that a shallow connection means a shallow loss. What he fails to recognize is that this strategy also guarantees shallow life, the very precaution against emotional devastation prevents the depth of connection that makes life meaningful.

Women partnered with counterdependent men face a particularly confounding situation because the man's behavior presents no obvious problems. He fulfills concrete obligations, rarely creates dramatic conflicts, and maintains general pleasantness. Yet the woman experiences a persistent sense of loneliness within the relationship, feeling that she lives alongside her partner rather than with him. When she attempts to articulate this dissatisfaction, the counterdependent man often responds with genuine confusion or defensiveness, pointing to his consistent presence and reliable behavior as evidence that the problem is her unrealistic expectations rather than his emotional unavailability. He may even feel resentful that his efforts at relationship participation go unappreciated, unable to recognize that he is providing the form of partnership while withholding its substance. The relationship continues in a state of permanent superficiality, intimate enough to prevent either partner from seeking connection elsewhere but never intimate enough to satisfy the fundamental human need for being truly known and accepted.

The Disorganized Attachment Legacy

For men whose early attachment experiences involved not just pressure toward premature independence but actual trauma, neglect, or inconsistent caregiving, the connection paradox takes an even more destabilizing form. These men develop what attachment researchers' term "disorganized attachment", a pattern characterized by the simultaneous activation of both approach and avoidance systems without any organized strategy for resolving the conflict. The disorganized man experiences connection as both desperately needed and potentially catastrophic, with no middle ground available. His nervous system registers intimate relationships as sources of both comfort and danger, triggering contradictory impulses that manifest as erratic, unpredictable behavior that confuses both him and his partner.

Research by attachment theorist Mary Main demonstrates that disorganized attachment in childhood predicts the most severe relationship difficulties in adulthood, precisely because the person has no coherent strategy for managing intimacy. The organized avoidant person at least has a consistent (if limiting) approach, maintain distance, minimize need, protect independence. The disorganized man has no such coherence. He may oscillate wildly between clinging desperation and hostile rejection within hours or even minutes. He might pursue intimacy aggressively while simultaneously sabotaging it through behavior guaranteed to drive the partner away. He experiences connection as essential while treating his partner as dangerous, creating a relational environment of sustained chaos that wears down even the most patient partners. The woman in a relationship with a disorganized man often describes feeling like she is "walking on eggshells," never knowing which version of him will appear, the vulnerable man desperately seeking reassurance or the hostile stranger who treats her with contempt.

What makes disorganized attachment particularly tragic is that the man himself experiences these oscillations as evidence that relationships are inherently unstable and dangerous rather than recognizing them as products of his own dysregulated attachment system. He may interpret his partner's exhaustion with his unpredictability as confirmation that people always leave, without connecting her departure to his behavior. He experiences his own contradictory impulses as rational responses to a partner who keeps "changing" rather than recognizing that his perception shifts based on whether his attachment or avoidance system is currently activated. Without therapeutic intervention specifically addressing the attachment disorganization, these patterns typically persist and intensify, with each relationship failure reinforcing the underlying belief that connection itself is intolerable.

The Reclamation of Interdependence

Understanding the paradox of masculine connection patterns points toward a radical reimagining of what healthy adult intimacy requires, particularly for men trapped in these defensive cycles. The path forward is not teaching men to overcome their need for independence; autonomy remains a legitimate psychological necessity but rather helping them recognize that genuine autonomy and deep interdependence are not mutually exclusive. The psychological maturity required for sustainable partnership involves what researchers' term "differentiated attachment", the capacity to maintain a clear sense of self while also depending significantly on intimate others, to need deeply without experiencing that need as threatening to identity or autonomy. This capacity requires men to fundamentally revise their understanding of what constitutes strength and masculine adequacy.

Therapeutic approaches addressing these patterns must go beyond generic communication skills or emotional literacy training to directly confront the shame men experience around dependency itself. Psychiatrist Richard Schwartz's Internal Family Systems model offers promise by helping men recognize their contradictory impulses around connection as competing protective strategies rather than evidence of character defects. The part that pursues intimacy and the part that sabotages it are both attempting to protect the person, one by meeting legitimate attachment needs, the other by preventing engulfment and abandonment. The goal is not eliminating either impulse but developing the capacity to recognize when defenses activate and choose responses based on adult reality rather than developmental programming. A man learning to notice "I am pulling away because intimacy is triggering engulfment panic" has already begun breaking the automatic pattern, even if he cannot immediately change his behavior.

Women navigating this paradox with partners can support change by recognizing withdrawal as defensive rather than personal, which allows for compassionate firmness rather than reactive pursuit or protective distance. When a man initiates his characteristic retreat, a response like "I notice you are pulling away right now, which tends to happen when we have been particularly close lately. I am not going anywhere, and this pattern does not have to control what happens between us" can interrupt the cycle by naming the defense without shaming it while also refusing to participate in the distancing. This approach requires tremendous emotional maturity from women, who must manage their own abandonment responses while maintaining a connection with a partner who is actively creating distance. Yet it remains one of the few interventions with demonstrated effectiveness in disrupting these deeply ingrained patterns. The man receives the corrective experience that connection does not inevitably lead to engulfment or abandonment, that his need does not render him unacceptable, and that interdependence can coexist with authentic autonomy. Over time, these experiences can begin rewiring the defensive architecture, allowing a man to approach intimacy as something other than an existential threat requiring constant management.

Chapter 7: Redefining Strength: From Control to Respect

The transformation from control to respect as the foundation of masculine strength represents one of the most difficult psychological migrations available to the modern man. This journey requires him to dismantle the very architecture that has organized his sense of power since boyhood, replacing coercive force with consensual influence, dominance with authority, and fear-based compliance with freely given regard. The difficulty lies not merely in learning new behaviors but in fundamentally reconceptualizing what strength means when it no longer involves the capacity to impose one's will on circumstances or people. For generations, masculine strength has been synonymous with control, control over one's environment, control over one's emotions, control over others' behavior, control over outcomes. This equation runs so deep in masculine psychology that questioning it feels like asking whether water is wet. Yet this very equation has become the primary source of masculine suffering in relationships where genuine partnership requires the surrender of unilateral control in favor of mutual influence, where strength must manifest not as the power to prevent others from affecting you but as the resilience to remain integrated while being affected.

The control-based model of strength developed from legitimate historical contexts where male competence was measured by the capacity to manage threats that could annihilate families and communities. A man who could not control his fear during a hunt, control his aggression within tribal hierarchies, control resource distribution, or control external threats to group survival represented a liability rather than an asset. This context created what anthropologist Richard Lee termed "tactical dominance", the legitimate exercise of control in specific high-stakes domains where unilateral decision-making capacity could mean the difference between survival and death. The problem emerged when this domain-specific competence became generalized into a totalizing worldview in which all scenarios, including intimate relationships, became arenas for demonstrating control. The man who could effectively control whether his family starved or survived translated that capacity into controlling how his wife dressed, controlling what his children believed, controlling the emotional tenor of household interactions, and controlling the terms of intimacy. What began as adaptive competence in genuine threat scenarios metastasized into a pervasive need to control all variables in all contexts, particularly those that activated anxiety about masculine adequacy.

Contemporary relationships expose the catastrophic limitations of control-based strength because intimate partnership fundamentally requires the ability to be influenced, to have one's perspective altered by another's needs and perceptions, to allow outcomes to emerge from negotiation rather than unilateral decision. When a man approaches a relationship through a control lens, he unconsciously transforms his partner into either an adversary to be defeated or a possession to be managed, both of which preclude actual intimacy. Research conducted by marriage therapist Terry Real documented what he terms "the control-connection paradox": the more a man attempts to control relational dynamics to reduce his anxiety, the less genuine connection becomes possible, which increases his anxiety and intensifies his attempts at control in a self-reinforcing cycle. The man who monitors his partner's friendships to control potential threats to the relationship thereby destroys the trust that makes the relationship worth protecting. The husband who controls financial decisions to maintain masculine provider status prevents his wife from experiencing him as a genuine partner rather than a benevolent dictator. The father who controls children's choices to ensure they reflect well on his parenting forfeits the opportunity for an authentic relationship in favor of performative success. In each case, the exercise of control defeats the very objectives it aims to achieve.

The Neurochemistry of Dominance Versus Authority

Understanding the distinction between control and respect requires examining how these different forms of social power operate at neurological and interpersonal levels. Control operates through dominance, the capacity to compel behavior through threat of negative consequences or withdrawal of resources. When a man exercises dominance in relationships, he activates his partner's threat-detection systems, triggering stress responses characterized by cortisol elevation, amygdala activation, and defensive mobilization. This produces compliance but not collaboration, obedience but not respect, fear-based submission but not freely chosen cooperation. The neuroscience of coercive control reveals that relationships organized around dominance maintain partners in a state of chronic low-level threat activation, where behavior is motivated by avoidance of punishment rather than pursuit of mutual benefit. Studies conducted by neuroscientist Stephen Porges on the polyvagal system demonstrate that threat-based relational dynamics prevent access to the social engagement system, the neural circuitry that enables genuine connection, collaborative problem-solving, and emotional attunement. When a woman's nervous system perceives her partner as a potential threat rather than a haven, her capacity for intimacy, sexual response, and emotional openness becomes neurologically compromised regardless of conscious intention.

Respect-based authority operates through entirely different mechanisms, activating what social psychologists' term "prestige hierarchies" rather than dominance hierarchies. Prestige derives from competence, consistency, integrity, and the freely offered regard of others who recognize valuable qualities and voluntarily defer to expertise or judgment. When a man earns respect rather than demanding compliance, his partner's nervous system remains in a state of safety that enables social engagement, and her deference to his judgment or leadership in particular domains emerge from genuine trust rather than fear. The critical distinction is that respect-based authority can be withdrawn the moment it is violated without catastrophic relational consequences, because the relationship is not organized around coercion. A woman who respects her partner's financial judgment can disagree with a specific decision without triggering defensive collapse, because her regard is based on demonstrated competence rather than enforced submission. The moment she complies out of fear rather than trust, respect has been replaced by dominance, regardless of what either party consciously believes about their relational dynamics.

The transition from control to respect requires men to tolerate profound vulnerability, because respect-based authority can be lost, whereas control-based dominance simply requires sufficient application of force. A man accustomed to controlling relational outcomes through emotional withdrawal, financial leverage, or implicit threats must learn to influence through persuasion, earn trust through consistency, and accept that his partner retains the autonomous capacity to reject his perspective or preferences. This feels terrifying to men whose sense of masculine adequacy depends on maintaining unilateral decision-making power. The capacity to say, "I disagree with your choice, but I respect your right to make it" requires psychological strength of an entirely different magnitude than the capacity to say "You will do this because I have decided." The former acknowledges the partner as a sovereign equal whose autonomy must be honored even when it produces outcomes he dislikes; the latter treats the partner as an extension of his will whose independent agency represents a threat requiring suppression.

Respect as Mutual Recognition

The philosophical concept of recognition, developed by theorist Axel Honneth, provides crucial insight into why respect represents a more sophisticated form of strength than control. Recognition involves acknowledging another person's inherent worth, their legitimate claims to autonomy and self-determination, and their capacity to hold valid perspectives that differ from one's own. When two people engage in mutual recognition, each confirms the other's full humanity while maintaining their own distinct subjectivity. This stands in stark contrast to control dynamics, where one person's subjectivity dominates while the other's gets subordinated or erased. Men socialized into control paradigms often experience their partner's autonomous subjectivity as a threat rather than a gift, interpreting her independent preferences, perspectives, and priorities as challenges to his authority that must be countered rather than as enriching differences that expand the relational field.

The poverty of control-based relationships becomes most visible in conflicts where genuine differences emerge that cannot be resolved through compromise. When a woman wants to accept a job opportunity that requires relocation and her partner wants to remain in their current city, control dynamics produce a zero-sum battle where someone's will must prevail and someone's will be defeated. The man operating from control paradigms experiences his partner's persistent advocacy for her preference as disrespect for his authority, interpreting her refusal to defer as a fundamental challenge to relational hierarchy. His psychological security depends on her eventual capitulation, not because his preference is objectively superior but because the relational structure requires clear winners and losers to confirm masculine dominance. Respect-based dynamics allow both parties to fully advocate for their legitimate needs while acknowledging the profound difficulty of a situation that threatens to leave someone's core needs unmet. The couple might ultimately decide based on whose career trajectory is more time-sensitive, whose family situation is more pressing, or whose psychological well-being would suffer most from the less-preferred option. Still, these considerations emerge from genuine negotiation between equals rather than the enforcement of hierarchical prerogative.

The capacity for mutual recognition requires what psychologists' term "mentalization", the ability to hold in mind that other people possess internal worlds as rich and legitimate as one's own, with desires, fears, histories, and needs that warrant consideration regardless of whether they align with one's preferences. Research conducted by developmental psychologist Peter Fonagy demonstrates that mentalization capacity varies dramatically between individuals and correlates strongly with relationship satisfaction and conflict resolution efficacy. Men with high mentalization capacity can genuinely engage with their partner's perspective even during intense disagreement, asking questions aimed at understanding rather than defeating her position, acknowledging the legitimacy of her concerns even while advocating for different solutions. Men with low mentalization capacity experience their partner's differing perspective as essentially incomprehensible or illegitimate, responding to her advocacy with dismissal, ridicule, or authoritarian insistence rather than genuine engagement. The low-mentalization man might say "That makes no sense" or "You're being irrational" when confronted with preferences that diverge from his own, because he literally cannot construct a coherent model of how a reasonable person could want something different than what he wants. His control-based framework provides no cognitive architecture for honoring autonomous subjectivity that produces inconvenient conclusions.

The Economic Roots of Control and Their Contemporary Erosion

The historical conflation of masculine strength with control emerged from economic arrangements where women's survival literally depended on male resource provision, creating material conditions in which male control was enforced through dependence. When a woman could not legally own property, could not access most forms of employment, could not obtain credit without a male co-signature, and would face social ostracism and likely destitution if she left an unhappy marriage, male control operated as much through economic coercion as through physical threat or ideological conditioning. Men exercised control not merely because they had been socialized to do so, but because economic structures made female compliance necessary for survival. The contemporary erosion of these economic dependencies, however incomplete, has exposed that much of what men experienced as respect was fear-based compliance that evaporated once women gained sufficient economic autonomy to choose their relational circumstances.

This economic transformation reveals the profound fragility of control-based masculine authority and explains much of the contemporary masculine crisis. Men who assumed their grandfather's level of unquestioned household authority would transfer automatically to their own relationships discovered that without economic coercion to enforce compliance, demands for obedience simply produced relationship dissolution. The capacity to financially support a family, which once automatically conferred decision-making authority, now represents merely one contribution among many rather than a trump card that settles all disputes. Men experience this shift as a loss of respect when it means the loss of coercive leverage that was mistaken for respect. True respect emerges only between parties who possess genuine alternatives, where deference is chosen rather than compelled. The woman who remains in a relationship because she wants to be there respects her partner in ways the economically trapped wife never could, because her presence represents active choice rather than absence of options.

Understanding this distinction helps women recognize when men's complaints about "lost respect" actually refer to lost control, and it allows men to recognize when their demands for respect actually represent demands for submission. When a man finds himself saying "She doesn't respect me anymore" after his partner has begun questioning decisions, voicing disagreement, or maintaining boundaries around his behavior, he is typically describing the loss of unilateral authority rather than the loss of genuine regard. Respect includes the capacity to disagree, to refuse, to maintain autonomous judgment. The woman who says "I respect your opinion, but I see this differently" or "I value your perspective and I'm going to choose another path" is demonstrating respect in its mature form, acknowledging his viewpoint as worthy of consideration while maintaining her own decisional autonomy. The man who experiences this as disrespect has confused respect with capitulation.

Building Respect Through Competence and Consistency

The pathway from control to respect requires men to develop entirely new sources of authority based on demonstrated competence, ethical consistency, and the accumulation of trust through reliable behavior over time. This represents far more difficult work than maintaining dominance, because respect must be continuously earned rather than enforced, and can be instantly lost through violations of integrity. Research conducted by organizational psychologist Amy Cuddy on the components of perceived trustworthiness reveals that people assess others along two primary dimensions: warmth (intentions toward others) and competence (ability to execute those intentions). Leaders who score high on both dimensions receive freely offered respect and willing followership; those who attempt to lead through authority assertion without demonstrated competence or benevolent intention produce resentment and resistance. In intimate relationships, men earn respect through consistent follow-through on commitments, expertise in domains their partner values, emotional regulation during conflict, protection of their partner's interests even when inconvenient, and the willingness to acknowledge mistakes and repair harm.

The competence component of respect building creates challenges for men because it requires them to actually be effective rather than simply claiming authority. A man cannot demand respect for financial stewardship while making poor investment decisions, cannot expect respect for emotional leadership while remaining emotionally dysregulated, and cannot command respect for problem-solving while consistently producing solutions that create more problems than they solve. This accountability strikes men accustomed to control paradigms as unfair, because dominance-based authority does not require demonstrated competence, it requires only the power to enforce compliance regardless of outcomes. The transition to respect-based authority means results actually matter, expertise becomes visible through outcomes rather than through assertion, and poor judgment reduces authority rather than being obscured through hierarchical position.

Men must accept that their partner's evaluation of their competence represents valid data rather than disrespect, that her refusal to defer to their judgment after repeated poor outcomes represents rationality rather than insubordination.

The consistency component requires men to maintain integrity between professed values and actual behavior, between promises and follow-through, between stated intentions and revealed priorities. Women track these consistencies with extraordinary precision because inconsistency signals untrustworthiness, and trusting an untrustworthy person creates danger. When a man repeatedly commits to behavioral changes during conflict but reverts to problematic patterns once tension subsides, his partner's respect erodes regardless of how compelling his explanations sound in the moment. When he advocates for equality in the relationship but consistently centers his needs and preferences over hers, his stated values lose credibility. When he presents himself as emotionally evolved but responds to criticism with defensive rage, the gap between performance and reality becomes undeniable. These inconsistencies do not represent mere hypocrisy; they reveal the difficulty of transforming deeply ingrained control patterns into genuinely respect-based relating. But recognition of the difficulty does not restore lost respect; only sustained consistency over time accomplishes that rebuilding work.

The vulnerability inherent in respect-based authority cannot be overstated. Unlike control, which can be maintained through force regardless of whether it produces good outcomes, respect evaporates the moment competence fails or integrity is violated. This makes respect-based masculine strength far more precarious and demanding than dominance-based strength, requiring constant attention to actual effectiveness rather than mere authority assertion. Men must accept that they will sometimes be wrong, that their partner's judgment may prove superior to theirs in particular domains, and that their authority in one area does not transfer to unrelated areas. That respect in a relationship must be perpetually renewed through continued demonstration of trustworthiness. This represents psychological labor of a magnitude most men have never been required to perform, and many experience the demand itself as emasculating because they have conflated masculinity with unquestioned authority rather than with earned trust.

The transformation from control to respect ultimately requires men to develop what philosopher Martha Nussbaum calls "capabilities", actual skills and capacities rather than positional authority or coercive power. A man's legitimate authority in a relationship should derive from his capability to provide genuine value: emotional regulation skills that create safety during conflict, financial acumen that genuinely improves family security, parenting wisdom that nurtures children's development, sexual generosity that prioritizes mutual pleasure, communicative precision that enables efficient problem-solving, and practical competence that addresses household needs. These capabilities command respect because they contribute tangible value that the partner recognizes and benefits from. The man who develops genuine capabilities earns respect that feels entirely different from the control-based compliance he may have previously mistaken for regard. His partner defers to his judgment in domains where his competence exceeds hers, not because she fears consequences of disagreement, but because she trusts that his expertise will produce better outcomes than her own guesswork in those specific areas. This willing deference, freely given and instantly revocable, represents the only form of respect compatible with genuine intimacy between equals.

The journey from control to respect does not make men weaker, it makes them stronger in ways that traditional masculinity cannot measure. The man capable of maintaining integration while his partner disagrees with him possesses a strength his grandfather never developed. The man who earns trust through consistency rather than demanding obedience through dominance operates from secure authority rather than fragile control. The man whose partner respects him because of who he is, rather than fears him because of what he can take away, lives in an entirely different psychological universe than the man whose authority depends on coercion. This transformation represents the essential developmental task for men who want genuine partnership rather than hierarchical subordination, connection rather than control, and strength that endures because it is freely recognized rather than reluctantly endured.

Chapter 8: The Role of Society: External Pressures and Expectations

The contemporary man does not merely inherit psychological patterns from his family or construct his identity solely through intimate relationships. He exists within a vast network of social surveillance systems that evaluate, judge, and enforce specific models of acceptable masculinity through mechanisms both brutally obvious and insidiously subtle. These external pressures function as a distributed disciplinary apparatus, operating through workplace hierarchies, peer group dynamics, media representations, consumer culture, digital social networks, and public space interactions to constantly monitor and correct masculine performance. The result is a man whose behavior in any given moment reflects not just his internal psychological state or his relationship dynamics, but his constant calculation of how that behavior will be perceived, judged, and potentially weaponized against his masculine status by the multiple audiences perpetually evaluating him. Understanding male behavior without accounting for these external pressures produces an incomplete and often misleading picture, attributing to individual psychology or relational dysfunction what represents rational adaptation to social surveillance systems that punish deviation from narrow masculine scripts with devastating efficiency.

The visibility of this surveillance varies dramatically by context, but its influence remains omnipresent. A man ordering a "feminine" drink at a bar with male colleagues faces immediate social penalties, mockery, exclusion from subsequent invitations, questioning of his sexuality, diminished status within the group hierarchy, that a

97

woman ordering a "masculine" drink would never encounter. This asymmetry reveals a critical truth about contemporary gender policing: while women face substantial pressures regarding appearance, behavior, and life choices, masculine policing operates with brutality around any behavior coded as feminine, because the fundamental crime in masculine culture remains not the violation of masculine norms themselves, but the contamination of masculinity with femininity. Research conducted by sociologist C.J. Pascoe on "fag discourse" in American high schools documented how the worst insult available to adolescent males, regardless of actual sexual orientation, invokes femininity, homosexuality, or weakness specifically because these categories represent masculinity's absolute boundary. The policing mechanism works not through encouraging excellence in masculine performance, but through terrorizing boys and men about proximity to anything feminine. This creates a psychological landscape where the primary masculine motivation becomes avoidance of the feminine rather than pursuit of any positive masculine ideal, producing the defensive, reactive quality that characterizes so much male behavior.

The Workplace as Masculinity Testing Ground

The professional environment functions as perhaps the most consequential arena of masculine evaluation, where economic survival, social status, and identity validation converge into a comprehensive measurement system that men navigate with constant vigilance. Contemporary corporate culture ostensibly embraces emotional intelligence, collaborative leadership, and work-life balance, but beneath this progressive veneer operates a ruthlessly traditional, masculine evaluation system that rewards aggression, availability, hierarchical dominance, and the performance of invulnerability. Studies conducted by organizational researchers Robin Ely and Debra Meyerson at Boston Consulting Group revealed that despite explicit policies supporting work-life balance and parental leave, men who actually utilized these policies faced substantial penalties in performance reviews, promotion decisions, and peer evaluations, not because their work quality declined, but because reducing work hours to accommodate family responsibilities violated implicit norms about masculine dedication and priorities. The men who advanced most rapidly maintained a performance of total professional availability even when policies theoretically permitted boundary-setting, effectively teaching younger men that the official rules and the actual rules governing masculine workplace success operate on entirely different principles.

This divergence between stated values and enforced norms creates impossible binds for men attempting to integrate personal development or relationship skills into their professional identities. A male manager who implements collaborative decision-making processes described in leadership training often finds himself perceived as weak or indecisive compared to more autocratic colleagues, despite research demonstrating superior outcomes from collaborative approaches. Men who speak openly about mental health struggles, parenting challenges, or work-life conflict, exactly the vulnerability that organizations claim to value, discover that such admissions mark them as unsuitable for leadership positions requiring the appearance of effortless competence. The man who leaves work at reasonable hours to attend his children's activities, exercises the paternity leave his company offers, or declines after-hours socializing to prioritize his marriage finds himself subtly excluded from the informal networks where real advancement decisions occur. These penalties rarely appear in formal evaluations and would be vigorously denied by the colleagues administering them. Still, they operate with sufficient consistency that most men learn to maintain a performance of traditional masculine priorities regardless of their actual values or personal needs. The cost of this performance extends beyond individual suffering into organizational dysfunction, as companies lose access to the full range of human capacity in their male employees while wondering why diversity and inclusion initiatives fail to produce authentic culture change.

The competitive dimension of workplace masculine evaluation deserves particular attention because it transforms colleagues into evaluators whose judgment directly impacts a man's economic survival and masculine status simultaneously. Unlike female workplace competition, which research by psychologist Joyce Benenson suggests often operates through reputation management and coalition formation, masculine workplace competition proceeds through more direct hierarchical contests over visible markers of dominance: who speaks longest in meetings, whose ideas receive attribution and adoption, who has access to powerful figures, who controls resources, whose authority goes unquestioned. These contests occur simultaneously on explicit levels, job titles, salary, office size, project assignments, and implicit levels involving constant micro-competitions over conversational dominance, physical space, deference patterns, and attention allocation. A man enters a conference room already calculating his position relative to other men present, adjusting his behavior based on where he falls in the status hierarchy, performing dominance toward lower-status males while showing appropriate deference to higher-status ones. This calculation happens largely beneath conscious awareness, operating as an automatic social positioning system that evolved to navigate male status hierarchies but creates exhausting vigilance in modern contexts where a man might participate in dozens of such hierarchical negotiations daily. The relational cost manifests when this competitive orientation prevents genuine collaboration or support, as helping another man could potentially elevate him above oneself in the hierarchy that determines masculine worth.

Digital Surveillance and Performance Metrics

The expansion of social media and digital communication has created unprecedented mechanisms for masculine surveillance and evaluation, transforming private behavior into public performance subject to constant documentation and judgment. A man's social media presence operates as a curated exhibition of masculine adequacy, where every image, statement, or interaction contributes to an overall impression that peers, colleagues, potential romantic partners, and even family members evaluate against internalized standards of acceptable masculinity. Research conducted by communications scholars at the University of Pennsylvania examining male Instagram usage patterns revealed distinctive patterns of masculine presentation: emphasis on achievement, adventure, athletic performance, and consumption; near-total absence of emotional vulnerability, domestic activities, or close male friendship displays; and consistent performance of stoic confidence regardless of actual life circumstances. These patterns replicate themselves across platforms with such consistency that they function as an informal masculine code, teaching men what aspects of their lives count as valuable enough for public display while others must remain invisible to preserve masculine credibility.

The metrics through which digital platforms operate, likes, followers, shares, comments, create quantified masculine evaluation systems more explicit than any previous era has produced. A man can now measure his masculine performance through precise numerical feedback, comparing his metrics against peers and adjusting his presentation to optimize for approval. This gamification of masculine identity produces peculiar distortions, as men increasingly construct experiences primarily for their documentation value rather than their intrinsic worth. The vacation chosen for its photographic potential rather than actual enjoyment, the expensive purchase displayed online to signal success, the carefully staged fitness photo demonstrating physical transformation, these represent experiences consumed primarily through their capacity to generate validation metrics rather than genuine satisfaction. Sociologist Erving Goffman's concept of "impression management" predates social media by decades, but digital platforms have intensified the self-monitoring they enable to unprecedented levels. Men now carry in their pockets devices that provide constant feedback about whether their masculine performance achieves sufficient approval, creating addictive feedback loops where self-worth becomes indexed to algorithmic validation. The consequences extend into intimate relationships as partners compete with the curated masculine identities men perform online, often discovering that the emotional energy invested in cultivating digital approval exceeds what remains available for actual human connection.

The anonymity certain digital platforms provide paradoxically reveals aspects of masculine psychology that face-to-face surveillance normally suppresses. Online gaming communities, anonymous forums, and comment sections frequently become spaces where men enact hypermasculine performances that would draw social sanctions in identifiable contexts, aggressive dominance displays, misogynistic language, threats toward perceived weakness, and rigid hierarchical enforcement. While it would be simplistic to claim these anonymous behaviors represent men's "true" selves. In contrast, their face-to-face courtesy represents mere performance; the disinhibition these spaces enable reveals fantasies of masculine power that civilized contexts require men to sublimate. Research by cyberpsychologist Mary Aiken examining online disinhibition effects demonstrates that anonymous digital contexts do not create new impulses but rather remove the social surveillance that normally regulates their expression, suggesting that the aggressive masculinity appearing in these spaces reflects desires that exist but remain constrained in observable contexts. This has profound implications for understanding male behavior in intimate relationships, as women often encounter versions of masculine aggression or dominance that seem inconsistent with their partner's public presentation, not recognizing that both represent genuine aspects of masculine psychology operating under different surveillance conditions. The man who appears emotionally intelligent at work, respectful in social contexts, and considerate in public spaces might still harbor fantasies of unilateral power that emerge in private relationship dynamics, not because he is deceptive, but because different contexts activate different aspects of the same complex masculine identity negotiating between internal desires and external expectations.

Economic Precarity and Masculine Worth

The connection between economic productivity and masculine value operates as one of society's most powerful and damaging equations, reducing a man's worth to his earning capacity in ways that women, while certainly facing economic pressures, rarely experience as fundamental to their gender identity. Research conducted by sociologists Kathryn Edin and Maria Kefalas on low-income communities documented how men who cannot fulfill provider roles often abandon family involvement entirely, rather than maintaining connection while economically marginal, not because they lack love for their children but because their presence without provision violates masculine identity so fundamentally that absence feels more coherent than failed presence. This pattern reveals the depth of the provider imperative in masculine psychology, it is not merely a role men perform but a prerequisite for legitimate masculine identity, such that economic failure disqualifies a man from manhood itself in his own assessment and often in the evaluation of the community around him. Contemporary economic conditions have made this equation catastrophic for millions of men, as deindustrialization, automation, and credential inflation have eliminated or devalued the forms of labor that previous generations of men used to establish masculine worth, while offering no alternative framework for deriving masculine value from non-economic contributions.

The psychological consequences of economic inadequacy for men differ substantially from those women experience during similar circumstances, precisely because masculine identity remains so thoroughly fused with economic productivity. A woman facing unemployment or underemployment experiences legitimate financial stress, anxiety, and diminished opportunity, but rarely experiences these challenges as disqualification from womanhood itself. A man in identical circumstances confronts not merely economic hardship but ontological crisis, if he cannot provide, what is he? The suicide rate among middle-aged men increased by forty-three percent between 1999 and 2017, according to data from the Centers for Disease Control and Prevention, with economic displacement and loss of traditional male employment serving as primary risk factors. These deaths represent not merely depression or mental illness in conventional terms, but the lethal consequences of identity collapse when the equation between economic productivity and masculine worth encounters circumstances that make that equation unsolvable. The tragedy intensifies because alternative sources of masculine value exist, caregiving competence, emotional availability, relational skill, community contribution, but these remain so thoroughly feminized in cultural imagination that many men cannot access them as legitimate bases for masculine identity even when they excel in these domains.

The intersection of economic precarity with relationship expectations creates additional pressures that women often fail to recognize because their own experience of economic stress operates differently. When a woman earns more than her male partner, research by sociologists Christin Munsch and Yue Qian demonstrates that the couple faces increased relationship instability, higher rates of infidelity by the male partner, and a greater likelihood of relationship termination, not because of practical conflicts over money, but because of threats to masculine identity that higher female earnings represent. The man whose partner out-earns him confronts daily evidence that he has failed the provider test, that his fundamental claim to masculine adequacy remains vulnerable to contradiction by his partner's superior economic performance. This creates desperate attempts to re-establish masculine hierarchy through other means, exercising control over non-economic decisions, withdrawing emotionally to demonstrate independence, or seeking validation through affairs that restore his sense of masculine desirability. Women experiencing these behaviors often interpret them as personal rejection or character defects, not recognizing them as symptoms of the economic inadequacy crisis playing out through relational channels. The societal solution cannot involve women diminishing their own economic advancement to protect male egos, but it requires recognition that until masculinity decouples from economic provision as its primary validation mechanism, men will continue experiencing female economic success as emasculating rather than as a partnership advantage.

The Physical Body as Masculine Currency

Physical appearance, fitness, and bodily presentation function as increasingly critical sites of masculine evaluation in contemporary culture, creating surveillance systems that subject male bodies to scrutiny previously reserved primarily for women. The rise of social media, fitness culture, and cosmetic industries targeting men has produced what researchers' term "the Adonis Complex", a syndrome of body image disturbance characterized by obsessive attention to muscularity, body fat percentage, and physical appearance that affects millions of men despite remaining largely invisible in cultural conversations about body image. Studies conducted by psychologist Harrison Pope examining male action figures from 1960 to the present documented dramatic increases in muscularity that now exceed even professional bodybuilders' proportions, teaching boys that normal male bodies represent failure rather than baseline adequacy. This muscular ideal creates an impossible standard, as achieving and maintaining the lean, heavily muscled physique now considered desirable requires either genetic advantages possessed by a small percentage of men or pharmaceutical enhancement through anabolic steroids that carry substantial health risks. Nevertheless, this standard operates as a critical component of masculine evaluation, with men whose bodies deviate facing mockery, exclusion, and erasure from desirable masculine categories.

The gym functions as a particularly revealing site of masculine body surveillance, where men engage in elaborate performances of physical dominance while constantly evaluating their own adequacy against peers. Unlike women's fitness contexts, which research suggests focus substantially on health, stress relief, and social connection, male gym culture operates primarily around competitive physical display, who lifts the heaviest weights, who possesses the most impressive physique, who demonstrates superior athletic performance. Men entering gyms report acute self-consciousness about body comparison and fears of judgment from more physically impressive males, creating anxiety that paradoxically undermines the stress reduction benefits exercise would otherwise provide. The toxic dimension of gym culture reveals itself in the prevalence of steroid use, which studies estimate affects fifteen to thirty percent of regular gym-going males despite serious health consequences, because chemical enhancement provides access to the muscular ideal that natural training cannot achieve. This represents men sacrificing literal health for the appearance of health, choosing endocrine disruption, cardiovascular risk, and psychological side effects over the masculine inadequacy that a normal body signifies in fitness culture. Women observing male gym behavior often interpret the intensity as admirable dedication or simple vanity, rarely recognizing the profound anxiety and compensatory status-seeking motivating men's compulsive physical development.

The sexual dimension of body surveillance deserves attention because it represents perhaps the arena where masculine physicality most directly translates into social power and status evaluation. Penis size operates as a source of pervasive masculine anxiety despite having minimal relevance to sexual function or partner satisfaction, because cultural discourse has transformed genital dimensions into a proxy for overall masculine adequacy. The ubiquity of pornography, which presents genital proportions far above population averages as standard, has intensified this anxiety for younger generations of men whose sexual education occurred substantially through pornographic images. Research examining male body image anxieties consistently finds genital size concerns ranking among the highest sources of physical inadequacy feelings, yet this remains a largely undiscussable anxiety because seeking reassurance would require admitting the vulnerability in ways that masculine culture prohibits. Men develop elaborate avoidance behaviors around contexts that might reveal genital size, gym locker rooms, intimate situations with new partners, medical examinations, despite the irrationality of the anxiety and the absence of actual negative consequences in most situations. This illustrates how masculine body surveillance operates largely through anticipated rather than actual judgment, as men's internal evaluation systems have internalized social standards so thoroughly that external enforcement becomes unnecessary.

The market forces capitalizing on masculine body anxiety have created entire industries around selling solutions to inadequacies that might not otherwise exist as problems. Male cosmetic surgery, hair restoration treatments, testosterone supplementation, penis enlargement procedures, and enhancement supplements together generate billions in annual revenue by exploiting and intensifying masculine physical insecurity. These industries operate through creating and then offering to solve problems, convincing men their bodies are inadequate in newly identified ways, then marketing expensive interventions as solutions. The parallel to the beauty industry's exploitation of female insecurity is obvious, yet male body surveillance has received substantially less critical attention despite growing rapidly in scope and impact. Men increasingly experience their bodies as projects requiring constant optimization, monitoring, and improvement rather than as simple vehicles for living, creating exhausting self-surveillance that displaces energy from relationships, personal development, and actual wellbeing. Women in relationships with men caught in these anxieties face partners whose physical insecurity infiltrates sexual intimacy, making what should be a connection instead become a performance evaluation where the man's focus on measuring his own adequacy prevents genuine presence.

The transformation of masculinity from an identity secured primarily through action and achievement into one increasingly dependent on physical appearance represents a fundamental shift with profound psychological implications. Previous generations of men could compensate for physical ordinariness through career success, wealth accumulation, social status, or character traits. Still, contemporary masculine culture increasingly treats physical appearance as a non-negotiable baseline requirement rather than one dimension among many. This shift has created a generation of men experiencing physical inadequacy as disqualifying regardless of other achievements, producing the bewildering phenomenon of professionally successful, financially secure men who nonetheless feel fundamentally inadequate because their bodies do not meet contemporary aesthetic standards. Understanding this pressure is essential for women attempting to comprehend why their partners might feel worthless despite apparent success, or why physical reassurance from partners often fails to mitigate body anxiety that stems from internalized cultural standards rather than actual partner judgment.

Chapter 9: The Journey to Authenticity: Embracing True Self

The transformation from performed masculinity to authentic selfhood represents not a single decision but a protracted negotiation between competing realities that occupy the same psychological space. A man begins this journey already fragmented, composed of the self he presents to colleagues, the self his family expects the self his partner believes she knows, the self that emerges in solitude, and beneath all these constructed versions, a nascent authentic self that has been systematically suppressed since early childhood. The journey to authenticity requires not discovering who he truly is, as popular psychology suggests, but rather deciding which of these multiple selves deserves priority when they inevitably conflict. This process differs fundamentally from feminine authenticity journeys, which typically involve integrating disparate aspects of self into coherent wholeness. Masculine authenticity more often requires strategic abandonment, consciously choosing to kill off performed versions of masculinity that have outlived their protective function but continue consuming enormous energy to maintain. The difficulty is that these performed selves are not mere costumes that can be removed at will. They have become neurologically embedded through decades of repetition, socially reinforced through networks of relationships built around the performance, and economically necessary in environments that punish authentic masculine vulnerability. A man cannot simply "be himself" when himself remains unclear and when being that unclear self risks annihilating the life structure he has spent years constructing.

Contemporary discourse around authenticity often treats it as an obviously superior state that anyone would naturally pursue once they recognized its benefits. This naive optimism ignores the profound costs that accompany masculine authenticity in a world still organized around traditional masculine performance. The man who begins expressing genuine uncertainty rather than projecting confidence discovers that clients, colleagues, and even friends start routing important decisions around him toward men who maintain the confidence performance, regardless of whether that confidence reflects actual competence. The father who admits to his children that he struggles with depression or anxiety, hoping to model emotional honesty, often finds that his honesty diminishes rather than enhances his authority in their eyes, because children, especially adolescent children, have internalized the same equations linking masculine worth to invulnerability that he is attempting to transcend. The husband who reveals the full extent of his sexual insecurity or performance anxiety to his wife, believing that intimacy requires radical honesty, may discover that his admission creates the exact attraction-destroying dynamic he feared, not because his wife consciously judges him as inadequate, but because her own desire has been conditioned by cultural scripts that eroticize masculine certainty. These consequences are real, not imagined. The man attempting authenticity must reckon with the genuine possibility that choosing to be himself might cost him relationships, professional opportunities, and social standing he cannot afford to lose.

The Authenticity Tax and Privilege Intersections

The costs of masculine authenticity distribute unevenly across racial, class, and educational lines in ways that discussions of male emotional development rarely acknowledge. A white professional man possesses access to therapeutic resources, progressive peer communities, and career flexibility that create safety nets for authenticity experiments. If expressing vulnerability costs him a promotion, other opportunities likely exist. If being emotionally honest strains his relationship, couples counseling remains available and affordable. If abandoning hypermasculine performance alienates certain friendships, he can cultivate new relationships in communities organized around alternative masculine values. Men without these resources confront far more brutal calculations. Research conducted by sociologist Alford Young at the University of Michigan, examining low-income Black men's identity negotiations, revealed that performing hardness, the presentation of emotional invulnerability and physical toughness, often represents a rational survival strategy rather than internalized toxicity. In neighborhoods were appearing vulnerable invites predation, where showing fear marks one as a victim, where admitting struggle suggests inability to protect one's family, authenticity becomes a luxury that only the economically secure can afford. The same performance that progressive discourse names as toxic masculinity may be the performance keeping a man alive, employed in sectors that reward aggressive dominance, and respected in communities where masculine codes operate by entirely different rules than those governing educated professional spaces.

Class intersections further complicate the authenticity journey in ways that women from any class background struggle to fully comprehend. Blue-collar work environments, particularly in construction, manufacturing, law enforcement, and military contexts, maintain masculine cultures that have remained substantially resistant to the emotional intelligence discourse that has penetrated white-collar professional settings. The factory worker or police officer attempting to integrate therapy insights about emotional vulnerability into his workplace persona confronts not merely disapproval but active hostility from colleagues whose economic survival depends on mutual adherence to masculine codes. These men police each other's performances ferociously precisely because any crack in the collective masculine armor threatens everyone's standing in hierarchies where reputation for toughness directly impacts who gets chosen for desirable assignments, who gets backed up in dangerous situations, and who commands respect from management. A man working construction who begins expressing feelings openly or questioning whether traditional masculine aggression serves him well may find himself systematically excluded from crews, assigned to less desirable jobs, or subjected to escalating tests designed to determine whether he has gone "soft." The social consequences extend beyond the workplace into communities where reputation established through work relationships determines broader social positioning. For these men, authenticity is not a self-optimization project but a form of social and economic suicide.

The racial dimensions of masculine authenticity present additional complexities that the predominantly white discourse around male emotional development systematically ignores. Black masculinity operates under entirely different surveillance regimes than white masculinity, where behaviors read as authentically expressive or healthily vulnerable when performed by white men become interpreted as threatening, unstable, or professionally inappropriate when performed by Black men. Research by psychologist Robert Sellers on racial identity and masculine performance documents how Black men learn to navigate what he terms "shifting", the constant adjustment of masculine presentation depending on the racial composition of the environment and the perceived threat level of the audience. A Black man's authentic self-expression in an all-Black space might involve verbal jousting, physical expressiveness, and emotional intensity that would trigger negative consequences if performed in predominantly white professional environments. The journey to authenticity for Black men, therefore, cannot simply mean expressing genuine feelings, because genuine expression itself becomes weaponized in racist evaluation systems that interpret Black male emotion as danger. The Black man who shows anger, even righteous anger about injustice, risks confirming stereotypes about Black male aggression. The Black man who shows sadness or hurts risks appearing weak in systems that already question Black male competence. The Black man who shows joy and exuberance risks being read as unprofessional or threatening. Authenticity under these conditions requires not merely internal emotional honesty but sophisticated calculation about which aspects of authentic self can be safely expressed in which contexts, a level of code-switching that white men's authenticity journeys rarely require.

The Disintegration Phase and Identity Dissolution

The path to authentic masculine selfhood nearly always passes through what therapists working with men in transition term "the disintegration phase", a period where the performed self begins crumbling faster than the authentic self can be constructed, leaving the man in a state of identity dissolution that resembles psychological free fall. This phase starts when a man can no longer sustain the energy required to maintain performed masculinity, often triggered by a crisis that exceeds his defensive capacity: divorce, job loss, serious illness, death of a parent, or betrayal by someone central to his identity structure. The crisis itself matters less than its effect of overwhelming the psychological immune system that has kept authentic feelings and needs suppressed. Suddenly, the performance fails. He cannot project confidence because he no longer believes it. He cannot maintain emotional stoicism because grief or fear has become too powerful to contain. He cannot fulfill provider or protector roles because circumstances have rendered him manifestly unable to provide or protect. The man experiences this not as liberation but as catastrophic disintegration, he is not discovering his true self but losing his only self, the only version of masculinity he has ever known how to perform. Panic typically follows, along with frantic attempts to restore the previous performance, but the disintegration cannot be reversed once begun. The defensive structures, once cracked, continue fragmenting despite his efforts to hold them together.

What makes this phase particularly treacherous is that the man looks functional to external observers even as he experiences internal dissolution. He continues going to work, fulfilling basic responsibilities, maintaining relationships, and performing the external markers of adult masculine competence. But internally, the coherent sense of self has shattered. He no longer knows what he actually feels versus what he has been conditioned to feel. He cannot distinguish genuine desires from performed desires. His values, previously experienced as obvious and natural, suddenly appear arbitrary or inauthentic. The behavioral scripts he has followed automatically for decades abruptly seem like someone else's lines that make no sense when examined closely. This creates a disorienting split between external continuity and internal chaos that partners and friends typically fail to recognize until the man's behavior becomes obviously erratic. Women who witness their partners entering this phase often interpret the changes as evidence of depression, midlife crisis, or relationship dissatisfaction. While these interpretations may have validity, they miss the deeper ontological crisis, the man is not merely sad or questioning his life choices but experiencing the dissolution of the only self-concept he has ever constructed. His authentic self, if it exists, remains so deeply buried under decades of performance that accessing it requires excavating through layers of defended masculinity that have become inseparable from his core identity.

The therapeutic interventions most offered during this phase, talk therapy focused on identifying feelings, mindfulness practices aimed at self-awareness, authenticity exercises designed to uncover true values, often prove inadequate because they assume the existence of a coherent self waiting to be discovered. But many men in the disintegration phase do not possess a cohesive self beneath the performance. The performance is all there has been. The work, therefore, is not an archaeological discovery but a creative construction, building a new masculine identity from raw materials that have never been assembled into an authentic form. This construction project has no blueprint, no clear endpoint, and no guarantee of success. The man must simultaneously abandon the familiar while building the unfamiliar, maintain functional adult responsibilities while experiencing psychological adolescence, and project enough stability to preserve key relationships while undergoing a transformation that makes him fundamentally unrecognizable to people who have known him for years. Many men fail this navigation, retreating into performed masculinity that now feels hollow but at least feels familiar, or rushing toward equally inauthentic alternative masculine performances that promise quick resolution to identity crisis, the spiritual seeker, the enlightened feminist ally, the stoic philosopher, the recovered addict, identities that offer new scripts rather than authentic self-construction.

Provisional Identity and Iterative Becoming

The actual construction of authentic masculine selfhood proceeds not through sudden revelation but through what developmental psychologists studying adult identity formation term "provisional identity adoption", trying on possible versions of self, testing them in real-world contexts, discarding elements that feel inauthentic, and gradually assembling a coherent masculine identity through iterative refinement. This process resembles scientific experimentation more than spiritual discovery. A man might provisionally adopt emotional expressiveness, sharing feelings more openly with friends and partners to determine whether this feels authentic or merely represents a different performance. The experiment generates data: How does it feel in his body to express emotion? Does it create desired connections or unwanted vulnerability hangovers? Do others respond in ways that feel affirming or threatening? Based on this experiential data, he adjusts the provisional identity, perhaps less expressiveness feels more authentic, or maybe the issue is not amount but context, or possibly he discovers that certain emotions feel authentic to express while others do not. Each iteration provides information about which aspects of masculine authenticity fit his temperament and circumstances versus which represent adoption of alternative masculine ideals that suit others but not him.

This iterative process confuses partners because the man's behavior and expressed values shift repeatedly as he tests different configurations of masculine selfhood. What he claims to want or believe in January may be contradicted by his behavior in March and explicitly rejected by June. Women interpret this as dishonesty, manipulation, or lack of commitment to change, unable to recognize it as necessary experimentation in someone learning to construct rather than perform identity. The provisional nature of each adopted stance is invisible to observers who reasonably assume that stated values and beliefs represent stable commitments rather than hypotheses being tested. When the man abandons a provisional identity that is not working, "I thought I wanted an open relationship but I realize I do not," "I believed I should prioritize career less but I feel empty without work intensity," "I tried therapy but talking about feelings makes things worse not better", his partner experiences betrayal or deception because she adjusted her own life and expectations based on his stated direction, not recognizing that direction was explicitly provisional. The man, meanwhile, experiences frustration that his honest experimentation gets interpreted as bad faith when he is working harder at authenticity than he has ever worked at anything. This fundamental incompatibility between iterative identity construction and relationship stability creates a bind: the process most likely to generate authentic masculine selfhood directly threatens relationship continuity because partners cannot build a stable partnership with someone whose core identity remains under construction.

The resolution to this bind requires something rarely achieved in practice, a meta-agreement about the authenticity project itself. Rather than the man expecting his partner to accept each provisional identity as if it were a permanent truth, he must explicitly negotiate the experimental nature of his identity construction. This means communicating not "I am now someone who values emotional openness" but rather "I am testing whether emotional openness feels authentic to me, and I need time to gather experiential data before knowing whether this represents genuine self versus adopted ideal." It means distinguishing between elements of self that have been verified through multiple iterations and can be relied upon versus elements still being tested. It requires the meta-cognitive capacity to observe and narrate one's own identity construction process while undergoing it, a level of self-awareness that many men lack and many relationships cannot accommodate, even when men possess it. Partners must decide whether they can sustain a connection with someone who is not yet finished, who may become someone quite different from what they expected, who needs permission to contradict himself as he learns who he authentically is. This is not a small request. It requires the partner to sacrifice her own need for stability and predictability while he conducts identity experiments that directly impact her life. Many women, reasonably, decline this sacrifice, particularly if they have already invested years in a relationship with the performed version of masculinity he now seeks to abandon.

The Social Cost of Non-Compliance

Perhaps the most overlooked dimension of masculine authenticity involves not what a man gains by being genuine but what he loses by refusing to perform traditional masculinity in contexts that demand it. Social systems organized around masculine hierarchies respond to non-compliance not with neutral acceptance but with active sanction designed to restore compliance or eliminate the non-compliant member from the system. A man who refuses to participate in workplace dominance performances finds himself excluded from informal networks where actual power operates, passed over for advancement opportunities, and ultimately pushed toward exit regardless of his technical competence. The man who declines to perform heterosexual masculine sexuality through locker room talk, strip club attendance, or sexual conquest storytelling faces questioning of his sexual orientation and systematic exclusion from male bonding activities that build social capital. The father who openly acknowledges struggling with parenting rather than projecting paternal authority discovers that other father's distance themselves, mothers question his judgment, and his children receive social feedback suggesting their father is inadequate. These sanctions are not imaginary persecution by a man overly sensitive to judgment. They represent structural enforcement mechanisms that maintain masculine hierarchies by making non-compliance socially and economically expensive.

Women often fail to recognize these sanctions because feminine authenticity, while certainly policed through different mechanisms, does not typically result in systematic exclusion from economic opportunity or social networks. A woman who rejects traditional feminine performance, who is not nurturing, not relationship-oriented, not communally focused, may face social disapproval but rarely finds her career systematically blocked or her competence questioned based on this gender non-compliance. The sanctions for masculine non-compliance operate far more comprehensively precisely because masculine hierarchies depend on collective compliance in ways that feminine social systems do not. If individual men begin opting out of dominance performances, hierarchy mathematics, and ranking systems that determine resource allocation, they will disintegrate. The system, therefore, mobilizes aggressive enforcement not because it is morally opposed to masculine authenticity but because widespread authenticity would destroy the evaluation systems that determine who succeed and who fails in male-dominated domains. Understanding this reveals why exhortations for men to simply "be authentic" ring hollow, authenticity is not forbidden because traditional masculinity is philosophically opposed to genuine selfhood, but because masculine hierarchies cannot function if men stop participating in the performances that enable ranking and resource competition.

The man attempting authenticity must therefore develop sophisticated dual consciousness, the ability to perform compliant masculinity when economic or social survival requires it, while maintaining a private, authentic identity that operates by different principles. This exhausting code-switching represents not failure to achieve authenticity but realistic navigation of systems that punish genuine masculine vulnerability and non-traditional masculine values. The executive who spends weekends in therapy excavating authentic feelings but Monday morning returns to performing decisive confidence is not hypocritical but pragmatic, he recognizes that the professional environment cannot yet accommodate the authentic uncertainty he is exploring privately. The father who discusses his parenting struggles with his therapist but projects traditional paternal authority to his children is not lying but protecting them from the social consequences of having a father marked as inadequate. This pragmatic authenticity, genuine in private spaces while performed in public domains, lacks the romantic purity that authenticity discourse often celebrates. Still, it represents the only viable path for most men whose economic survival and social positioning depend on contexts that demand traditional masculine performance. Women who insist that authentic masculine selfhood must be consistently expressed across all contexts without regard for consequences often reveal their privilege, they can advocate for others' authenticity without bearing the costs that authenticity would impose on their partners' careers and social standing. The man lives those costs daily and makes rational calculations about when authenticity can be afforded and when performance remains necessary.

Chapter 10: Bridging the Gap: Building Empathy and Clarity

The construction of functional empathy between men and women requires abandoning the fantasy that understanding produces automatic harmony. A woman can achieve profound comprehension of masculine psychology, its developmental origins, defensive structures, communication patterns, and relational limitations, while simultaneously experiencing legitimate frustration, disappointment, and anger about how these patterns impact her life. Empathy is not agreement. It does not require accepting behavior as unchangeable simply because its origins make sense. The critical distinction involves recognizing that understanding why a man operates in ways creates strategic leverage for effective response, not moral obligation to accommodate dysfunction. This chapter addresses the practical architecture of bridging relational gaps between men and women through clarity that serves both parties, empathy that maintains boundaries rather than dissolving them, and communication strategies that work with masculine psychology rather than against it. The goal is not creating perfect mutual understanding, an impossible standard that sets up inevitable failure, but rather developing sufficient functional literacy in each other's psychological languages to navigate conflict, negotiate needs, and build relationships that honor both parties' legitimate requirements without demanding either person fundamentally transform their neurological wiring or abandon their gendered socialization.

The prevailing discourse around heterosexual relationship improvement places responsibility primarily on men to develop emotional capacity that matches feminine standards, framing masculine communication limitations as deficits requiring correction rather than differences requiring navigation. This framework, while identifying real problems in male emotional development, creates a dynamic where women wait for men to become fluent in feminine relational languages before functional connection becomes possible. The wait often extends indefinitely, producing resentment on both sides, women feeling perpetually disappointed by men who cannot meet reasonable emotional needs, men feeling perpetually inadequate, no matter how much therapeutic work they complete. A more productive framework acknowledges that while men benefit enormously from expanding emotional literacy and reducing defensive patterns, women simultaneously benefit from learning to communicate in ways that work with rather than against masculine psychological architecture. This is not about women lowering standards or accommodating masculine limitations, but rather about developing bilingual capacity that allows both parties to be met where they actually exist rather than where ideology suggests they should exist. The distinction matters enormously: learning to communicate effectively with men as they are does not prevent also expecting men to grow; it simply recognizes that growth occurs more readily when communication works rather than when it perpetually fails due to format incompatibility.

Strategic Empathy and the Observational Stance

The empathy women need to cultivate toward men differs substantially from the emotional empathy that characterizes feminine friendship patterns, where empathy involves feeling with another person, experiencing their emotional state as a form of resonance, and providing presence that validates suffering. This form of empathy, while valuable in many contexts, often proves counterproductive when applied to masculine psychology because it triggers the defensive reactions explored in previous chapters while simultaneously depleting the woman's emotional resources through absorption of pain she cannot actually resolve. Strategic empathy operates differently, maintaining what therapists call "the observational stance", a position of curious inquiry that seeks to understand the machinery producing behavior without merging emotionally with the person's experience or taking responsibility for fixing their internal state. When a woman observes her partner exhibiting defensive withdrawal after a moment of vulnerability, strategic empathy asks, "What function is this withdrawal serving for him?" rather than "How can I make him feel safe enough to stay open?" The first question maintains appropriate boundaries around whose problem requires solving, while the second unconsciously assumes responsibility for managing his regulatory capacity, which inevitably fails and produces resentment.

The observational stance requires cultivating what Buddhist psychology terms "near enemies", states that superficially resemble positive qualities but undermine them. The near enemy of empathy is pity, and the near enemy of compassion is enabling. Women socialized toward caretaking often confuse supporting men's growth with protecting men from consequences, interpreting strategic withdrawal of support as cruelty rather than recognizing it as the intervention most likely to motivate change. Research conducted by psychologist Harriet

Lerner on relationship systems demonstrates that the most effective intervention when facing a partner's persistent dysfunctional pattern involves clearly articulating the problem, explaining its impact, stating what must change, then allowing the partner to experience natural consequences of not evolving rather than continuously accommodating the dysfunction while expressing frustration about it. This approach feels harsh to many women because it violates feminine socialization toward smoothing relational friction and maintaining connection even at personal cost. However, the alternative, continuing to function in ways that allow men to avoid confronting their limitations, ensures those limitations persist indefinitely. Strategic empathy understands masculine psychology well enough to know that men change through crisis more reliably than through encouragement, through confronting actual consequences more than through processing feelings about potential impacts, and through experiencing a partner's genuine limit rather than her theoretical limit that proves negotiable when tested.

Implementing the observational stance requires women to develop tolerance for their own discomfort during a partner's struggle. When a man encounters a situation requiring emotional capacity he has not created, the feminine impulse often involves jumping in to do the emotional labor for him, explaining to him what he is feeling, teaching him how to express it, managing the social situation he is bungling through incompetence. Strategic empathy recognizes these rescue operations as precisely the pattern that has prevented him from developing the capacity in the first place. The more effective intervention involves witnessing his struggle, acknowledging its difficulty, and maintaining a firm expectation that he navigate it himself, even if his navigation is clumsy and imperfect. A man who has always had women explain his own feelings to him never develops the neural pathways required to do this work independently. A man who has never had to sit with another person's anger or disappointment without being rescued from it by feminine emotional management never learns to regulate his own defensive reactions. The observational stance is not passive, it involves active witnessing, clear feedback about impact, and firm boundaries about what is acceptable, but it refuses the caretaking role that enables continued masculine emotional underdevelopment while exhausting the women who perform it.

Precision Language and Masculine Translation

The communication gap between men and women persists not primarily because of what is said but because identical words carry different semantic and emotional weight depending on who speaks to them. When a woman says, "We need to talk," she is typically inviting collaborative sense-making through conversation. When a man hears, "We need to talk," his nervous system interprets an imminent performance evaluation that will likely reveal his inadequacy. The words are identical; the meaning is radically divergent. Bridging this gap requires women to develop what might be termed "masculine translation capacity", the ability to encode relational needs and emotional content in formats that work with masculine psychology rather than triggering its defensive systems. This is not about manipulating men or speaking in code, but rather about understanding that directness means different things in masculine versus feminine communication cultures. In feminine contexts, indirect communication that allows the listener to save face and maintain relational harmony is often the most direct path to actual behavioral change. In masculine contexts, indirect communication reads as ambiguity requiring interpretation, which most men lack the emotional literacy to perform accurately, leading them to guess wrong and then feel accused of willful misunderstanding when they guess wrong.

Masculine translation prioritizes several key principles that feel unnatural to women habituated to feminine communication norms. First, lead with the specific request rather than the emotional context. Instead of, "I feel disconnected from you lately and I miss the closeness we used to have and I worry that we are drifting apart and I want us to prioritize time together," masculine translation produces, "I need us to schedule one night per week for just the two of us with no screens. Can you commit to Thursdays?" The second version feels abrupt and transactional to feminine sensibilities, but it provides the action-oriented clarity that masculine psychology can actually process and implement. The emotional context, feeling disconnected, missing closeness, worrying about drifting, can be added briefly after the request has been made and agreed to, but leading with emotional context buries the actual request under information that men's nervous systems interpret as evidence of a problem without a clear solution, which triggers defensive reactions rather than cooperative engagement, second, separate observation from interpretation. Masculine psychology responds far better to factual descriptions of observable behavior than to interpretations of internal states that men experience as mind-reading. "You have cancelled our last three planned date nights" works better than "You do not prioritize our relationship," even though the woman may legitimately interpret the pattern as evidence of deprioritization. The first statement is disprovable only through denial of factual reality; the second is disprovable through challenging her interpretation of his internal motivation, which immediately derails the conversation into debates about unknowable internal states rather than addressing the observable pattern.

Third, attach explicit timelines and success metrics to requests for behavioral change. The feminine communication pattern of making requests through an implicit expectation that a sensitive partner would simply know what is needed systematically fails with masculine psychology, not because men are insensitive, but because they lack the emotional pattern recognition that would allow them to infer unstated needs from contextual clues. "I need you to be more emotionally available" contains no implementable information for most men, what specific behaviors constitute emotional availability? How frequently? In what contexts? Measured by what standard? Masculine translation produces, "I need you to check in with me about how I am doing at least twice per week through questions that are not just logistics, and when I share something difficult, I need you to listen for at least five minutes before offering solutions." This level of specificity feels absurdly mechanical to women accustomed to relational attunement that flows naturally rather than through explicit instruction, but it provides the concrete behavioral guidance that allows men to actually comply with the request rather than failing through lack of clarity about what success looks like. Fourth, deliver critical feedback in contexts that minimize status threat. The masculine sensitivity to status and competence means that feedback delivered publicly or in contexts where the man is already feeling inadequate will trigger maximum defensiveness regardless of how gently it is delivered. Feedback delivered privately, in contexts where the man feels generally competent, and framed as information rather than judgment, has a far higher probability of being received and processed. This means that the moment when a man has just bungled an emotional situation is precisely the wrong moment to explain how he bungled it; waiting until he is regulated and receptive produces far better outcomes, even though the feminine communication culture values immediate processing while feelings are fresh.

Graduated Disclosure and the Trust Ladder

One of the most common patterns undermining heterosexual relationships involves women expecting men to demonstrate emotional vulnerability at levels that require trust men do not yet feel. The feminine socialization toward rapid intimacy and extensive disclosure creates expectations that men should be able to share their deepest fears, shames, and wounds relatively early in relationships or during conflicts where such disclosure would supposedly facilitate resolution. However, masculine psychology operates through what therapists working with male trauma survivors' term "graduated disclosure", a slow, incremental process of revealing vulnerability only after extensive testing has confirmed that the disclosure will not be weaponized, dismissed, or used as evidence of masculine inadequacy. Women who insist on deep disclosure before this trust has been established do not obtain honest sharing; they obtain performed vulnerability that tells them what they want to hear while protecting the man's actual vulnerable content from exposure to an insufficiently trustworthy audience. Understanding this pattern allows women to build what might be called "the trust ladder", a systematic approach to earning access to deeper levels of masculine vulnerability through demonstrated safety at shallower levels.

The trust ladder operates through behavioral proof rather than verbal reassurance. Men do not believe women will keep their vulnerability safe because women promise to keep it secure; they think it after they have disclosed something vulnerable and watched carefully to see what the woman does with that information. Did she bring it up later during an argument as evidence of his inadequacy? Did she tell friends or family, violating the implicit confidentiality that men require around vulnerable disclosure? Did she become anxious or uncomfortable, signaling that his vulnerability triggered her own fears about his adequacy? Did she respond with problem-solving that dismissed the emotional content in favor of solutions, confirming his suspicion that his feelings are problems requiring fixing rather than experiences deserving witness? Any of these responses confirms masculine fears that vulnerability is dangerous and will be used against him, which closes down access to deeper layers, potentially for years. Conversely, when a woman receives vulnerable disclosure with calm acknowledgment, maintains strict confidentiality, resists the urge to problem-solve unless explicitly asked, and later demonstrates through her behavior that the disclosure has not altered her fundamental respect for his competence, she earns access to the next rung of the vulnerability ladder. This process cannot be rushed. It requires patience that many women find frustrating, particularly when they have already demonstrated their own vulnerability extensively and expect reciprocity.

The graduated disclosure framework requires women to recognize that vulnerability is not binary but exists along a spectrum from relatively safe surface disclosures to extremely dangerous core disclosures. Many men can relatively easily disclose worry about work performance, frustration with friends, or anxiety about aging parents, these represent vulnerable content but do not threaten core masculine identity. The same men may require years of demonstrated safety before they can disclose sexual insecurity, fear of being a bad father, terror about financial inadequacy, or shame about their bodies. Women who push for deep disclosure before sufficient trust exists communicate through that very move that they do not understand masculine psychology well enough to be trusted with its most defended content. The push itself becomes evidence that the woman prioritizes her need for intimacy over his need for safety, which paradoxically prevents the intimacy she seeks. More effective approaches involve explicitly acknowledging the graduated nature of vulnerability: "I recognize that sharing this requires tremendous trust. I will not push you to share more than you feel safe. What I need from you is acknowledgment that this conversation needs to happen eventually, and some sense of what would help you feel safe enough to have it." This approach respects masculine defensive structures while maintaining a clear expectation that growth toward greater vulnerability remains necessary, creating a middle path between demanding immediate disclosure and indefinitely accommodating emotional unavailability.

Repair Protocols and the Rupture-Recovery Cycle

Perhaps the most critical capacity for bridging gaps between men and women involves developing effective repair protocols after relational ruptures occur. Ruptures, moments when one party hurts the other through action or inaction, when conflict escalates beyond productive bounds, when trust gets violated, are inevitable in intimate relationships. The quality of the relationship is determined not by whether ruptures occur but by whether effective repair follows them. Research conducted by relationship scientist John Gottman demonstrates that relationship satisfaction correlates more strongly with repair attempt success rate than with conflict frequency, conflict intensity, or even overall compatibility. Yet masculine and feminine approaches to repair operate on such different principles that they often function as mutual sabotage rather than reconciliation. Women typically initiate repair through emotional processing, an extended conversation that names the hurt, explores its origins, examines each party's contribution, and reestablishes emotional connection before moving forward. Men typically attempt repair through behavioral correction, identifying what went wrong, committing to different future behavior, and demonstrating that commitment through action rather than extended discussion. Neither approach is inherently superior, but their incompatibility creates situations where both parties attempt repair in good faith. Yet, both feel the attempt fails because it does not follow the repair protocol they need.

Effective repair protocols for male-female relationships require hybrid approaches that honor both partners' repair requirements rather than forcing all repair into one person's preferred format. This means women must become willing to accept behavioral repair as legitimate, even when it feels insufficient compared to emotional processing. At the same time, men must develop the capacity for enough emotional processing to address the woman's repair requirements, even when extended conversation feels redundant or performative. A functional hybrid protocol might proceed as follows: First, both parties agree that a rupture has occurred and that repair is necessary. This agreement need not involve extensive emotional processing at the outset, simply acknowledging "we hurt each other and we need to fix it" establishes shared commitment to repair. Second, the woman articulates her experience of the rupture in emotion-focused language, while the man listens without defending or problem-solving. The goal here is not for him to fully comprehend her emotional experience, which may be developmentally beyond his current capacity, but simply to hear that the rupture created genuine pain. Third, the man articulates his understanding of his contribution to the rupture in behavior-focused language, what specific actions or inactions caused harm. This allows the woman to assess whether he grasps what actually went wrong, which is essential for trusting that future behavior will differ.

Fourth, the man proposes specific behavioral changes that will prevent repetition of the rupture. This satisfies the masculine need for action-oriented resolution while providing the woman with concrete evidence of commitment to change. Fifth, the woman either accepts the proposed changes as sufficient or explains what additional changes are necessary, maintaining focus on observable behavior rather than internal states. Sixth, both parties agree on a timeline for reassessment, when will they check whether the behavioral changes have been successfully implemented? This prevents the repair from becoming a one-time conversation that never gets revisited, which allows men to believe the issue is resolved when behavioral change has not actually occurred. Seventh, and often most difficult for both parties, they practice what relationship therapist Esther Perel terms "productive closure", they explicitly agree that the rupture has been adequately addressed for now, which allows both people to move forward without the woman continuing to process the rupture past the point of useful extraction of meaning and without the man believing the issue is permanently resolved when the woman still carries unprocessed hurt. This final step requires tremendous discipline from both parties: the woman must resist her urge to continue processing until she feels completely satisfied, recognizing that complete satisfaction may never arrive and that continuing to discuss the rupture past the point of new insight being generated becomes counterproductive. The man must resist his urge to declare the matter finished prematurely, recognizing that his discomfort with emotional processing does not mean the processing has been sufficient.

The most sophisticated repair capacity involves meta-communication about the repair process itself, discussing not just the rupture but how the couple attempts to repair ruptures and whether those attempts work for both parties. This creates space to negotiate repair protocols that honor both people's needs rather than fighting about whose repair style is correct. A woman might say, "I notice that when we fight, you want to fix the problem quickly, and I want to talk about feelings more. Can we agree that we will do twenty minutes of my kind of repair followed by twenty minutes of your kind of repair?" This explicit negotiation transforms repair from a power struggle about whose protocol wins into collaborative problem-solving about how to serve both partners' legitimate repair requirements. Similarly, men can advocate for their repair needs without dismissing feminine requirements: "I hear that you need more emotional processing than feels natural to me. I am willing to work on developing more capacity for that. What I need from you is acknowledgment when I am stretching beyond my comfortable range, and patience when I hit my limit and need to take a break before continuing." This kind of meta-communication requires both parties to view their conflicting repair styles as problems to solve together rather than evidence that the other person is doing relationships wrong.

The repair process also requires understanding what relationship researcher Sue Johnson terms "attachment injuries", ruptures that threaten the fundamental security of the relationship bond rather than just causing temporary hurt. Attachment injuries occur when one partner is emotionally unavailable during a moment of dire need, when trust is violated in ways that call the entire relationship's safety into question, or when core relationship agreements are broken. These injuries cannot be repaired through the standard protocols that work for ordinary ruptures; they require more intensive intervention, often involving explicit recommitment to the relationship, extended rebuilding of trust through consistent behavior over time, and usually therapeutic support to process the injury's impact. Men frequently fail to distinguish between ordinary ruptures and attachment injuries, treating catastrophic betrayals as though they should be resolved through the same quick behavioral correction that works for minor conflicts. Women, conversely, sometimes treat ordinary ruptures as attachment injuries, responding to common conflicts as though they threaten the relationship's fundamental security when they actually represent normal relational friction. Developing shared capacity to distinguish between rupture types allows couples to calibrate their repair efforts appropriately, bringing sufficient intensity to genuine attachment injuries while not overwhelming ordinary conflicts with crisis-level response.

Understanding masculine psychology from the comprehensive perspective this book has provided creates the foundation for building bridges across seemingly unbridgeable gaps. Women equipped with this understanding can choose their battles strategically rather than fighting all masculine limitations simultaneously, can communicate in formats that work with rather than against male neurological architecture, can calibrate their empathy to protect their own resources while still supporting growth, and can negotiate repair protocols that serve both parties rather than privileging one person's relational style. This is not about excusing masculine dysfunction or accepting permanent limitation, but rather about working effectively with the raw material that actually exists rather than the ideal material that ideology suggests should exist. The man sitting across from you is not a blank slate ready to be molded into feminine relational ideals; he is a person shaped by specific developmental history, operating with specific psychological architecture, navigating specific social pressures, and possessing specific capacities and limitations. Meeting him where he actually is, with a clear-eyed understanding of both his potential and his constraints, creates the only viable foundation for functional connection and sustainable relationship. The alternative, demanding he become someone fundamentally different before genuine partnership becomes possible, ensures perpetual disappointment for both parties and prevents the actual growth that becomes possible when understanding replaces judgment, strategic intervention replaces rescue, and collaborative navigation replaces unilateral expectation.

About The Author

Megan T. Rios is a passionate advocate for emotional literacy and gender dynamics. Holding a master's degree in psychology and a background in social work, she has spent over a decade working with individuals and couples to foster deeper understanding and communication. Her expertise lies in breaking down barriers to emotional expression and promoting empathy between genders. Having lived experiences that echo the themes of this book, Megan blends academic insights with real-world narratives, making her uniquely suited to explore the complexities of modern masculinity. She is a sought-after speaker and workshop leader, helping many navigate the often tumultuous waters of relationships in contemporary society. Through 'The Book On Men (for Women),' Megan aims to empower women to understand the men in their lives while encouraging men to embrace vulnerability and connection.

About The Publisher

Welcome to The Book On Publishing

At The Book On Publishing, we believe in rewriting the rules of learning. Whether you're chasing your next big idea, building a better life, or simply curious about what should have been taught in school, you've come to the right place.

We're a platform built for dreamers, doers, and lifelong learners, offering bold, practical books and tools that empower you to take charge of your journey. From real-world skills to mindset mastery, we publish the book on what matters.

No fluff. No lectures. Just what you need to know, delivered with clarity, purpose, and a spark of curiosity.

Start exploring. Start growing. Start writing your story.

Read more at https://thebookon.ca.

Acknowledgment of AI Assistance

Portions of this book were developed with the support of
AI. While every word has been carefully reviewed and
refined by the author, AI served as a valuable tool for
brainstorming, editing, and structuring ideas. Its assistance
helped accelerate the creative process and clarify complex
topics.

www.ingramcontent.com/pod-product-compliance
Lightning Source LLC
Chambersburg PA
CBHW060237030426
42335CB00014B/1499